An ATHEIST, DRUG DEALER, and a RABBI...

A Redemption Story
from Generation to Generation

IRA BRAWER

SILVERSMITH
PRESS

Published by Silversmith Press—Houston, Texas
www.silversmithpress.com

ISBN 978-1-961093-89-8 (Hardcover Book)
ISBN 979-8-987381-68-7 (Softcover Book)
ISBN 979-8-987381-69-4 (eBook)

To my best friend and partner in life, Gloria
our children Sammi, Seth, Josie, Micha and Avi
our grandchildren, Jordan, Joshua, Joseph, Kaylee,
Tirzah, Noa, Shiloh, Ilan, and Libi
and those who are yet to come!

"One generation will praise Your works to another
and declare Your mighty acts."
Psalm 145:4

CONTENTS

CHAPTER 1
SHE'S CRAZY

1983. Estes Park, Colorado

"I'm born again," Gloria announced as she bounded into the house. I had heard the term before. Jimmy Carter made it famous a few years prior in his interview with *Playboy* magazine, of all things! But I really didn't know what it meant, except it was some Christian thing.

All I knew was I wasn't interested and made that clear: "I'm Jewish. Jews don't believe in Jesus, so don't bother me with that Jesus stuff, I'm not interested. End of story!"

Gloria was raised Southern Baptist, but only started going to church regularly as an adult since our AA involvement. The next words out of her mouth were slightly alarming, "And I want you to be *also!*"

My first reaction was, *That's okay for you—after all you're a Gentile ...* but then I thought, *Does this mean we have to get a divorce?* We had only been married for about six months. Gloria had been going to church as part of her twelve-step program which started eighteen months prior, while I had been going to Alanon meetings. The counselors talked about the idea of "God, as you understand Him"—which was already a stretch for me. I was okay with that though, but not this Jesus thing.

I was actually an atheist when I showed up for family week in Jordan, Minnesota, a couple of years earlier, where Gloria was

1

on rehab for drugs and alcohol. While I had a long history at that point of drug and alcohol abuse, starting right after high school, I was certainly not an "addict." At that point I was fresh off a divorce from Judy, my first wife with whom I had two children, Sammi and Seth.

Gloria and I were enjoying the party life of sex, drugs, and rock and roll, when a friend had recognized the pattern of addiction in Gloria and convinced her to go for treatment. So here I am going to family week to learn about the dangers of alcohol, and I'm being challenged by a counselor to believe in God "as you understand Him."

As an atheist that seemed silly. *How can I "understand Him" if I don't believe that "He" exists?*

But she confronted me with the question, "Can you believe that there is something outside yourself to believe in, even if it's a tree?"

At that point I thought, *okay, maybe there is something outside myself to believe in. I can believe in a tree.* Sounds silly now, of course, and I nodded in agreement.

She ended our session with, "And, by the way, it won't work if you stay with Gloria, and continue to drink and use drugs."

That was a huge turning point in both of our lives. At that time, we had been living together for a couple of years and were comfortable. I was a prominent member of the community. I had my own real estate company in Estes Park, a beautiful town situated in the Rocky Mountains and a gateway to Rocky Mountain National Park. I was president of the local Board of Realtors, and at one time, president of the local Chamber of Commerce. I was active in the community, in various civic clubs.

About a year after her treatment started, on August 1, 1982, Gloria and I were married at the famous Stanley Hotel in Estes Park by a Unitarian minister, who was a friend of ours. The one condition I requested was, "Please, no mention of God in the wedding!" to which he agreed. It was a beautiful wedding, with my two children, Sammi and Seth as part of the wedding, and our families coming in from out of town—which is a story in its own right. You see, Gloria was raised in a small town in Mississippi, while I was raised in New York City. Our cultural upbringing was as different as night and day. Both of her parents spoke with a strong southern accent, while my parents, being immigrants from Germany and Austria, spoke with a strong German accent. But everyone seemed to get along, even if they didn't understand each other too well.

The cultural differences between us at first seemed novel but would prove to be challenging in our relationship in the days and years to come. But what would prove to be even more challenging would be the "baggage" that we each unknowingly brought into the marriage. I had been divorced once already, and my parents were divorced, so my internal expectations for "lasting love" were hit or miss. Besides that, Gloria had been sexually abused by her grandfather and uncle, so, deep down, her trust of men was very low. Without really being aware, we both carried deep hurts and wounds from the past and had a false belief that marriage was going to make us happy and fulfilled—after all, we dearly loved each other and that was all that was needed. Or so we thought in our blissful naivety.

We had no idea that our marriage would bring out the worst in each of us by design, so we could deal with our stuff and grow. So, with our internal wounds bumping up against each other, we encountered problems almost from the start including infidelity, financial hardship, and now this conflict over the spiritual issue. Of course, I just thought I married a crazy woman. But I loved her madly none the less.

Could this marriage survive? Time to start seeing if that tree or "God as I understood Him" could help. Thus began my faith journey.

CHAPTER 2
A LONG LINE OF RABBIS

In reality, my faith journey started much longer ago, before I was born. My grandmother always told us that we came from a long line of rabbis, but growing up we just thought it was her wishful thinking. However, as an adult doing research on our family lineage, I found that indeed there was a line of rabbis in the family, apparently important ones, going back to the 1500s.

PERSECUTION AND EXPULSION

During the first Crusade in 1096, following the massacre of Jews by the crusaders, many Jews moved from western and central Europe to Provence, a region in France where there was protection for a time. The rabbis that flourished there were known as the "Wise Men of Provence."

The Jews were expelled from Provence by King Philipe Le Bel in 1306. Some moved to Portugal, including Rabbi Avraham Chayut, one of the leaders of this movement. In 1492, the Jews of Spain were forced to either convert to Christianity, leave, or be killed. This was part of the Spanish Inquisition, initially established to root out "heresy" from within the Catholic church. It became a tool of persecution and murder for Jewish people. Many did convert but secretly kept their Jewish practices. They were, and still are, called *morranos*, a derogatory name, meaning "pigs." If found out, they faced interrogation, torture, and possible death if they didn't' "repent" and renounce their Jewish practices. Many of them fled to Portugal. But a few years later, in 1506, as a condition for marrying the Infanta Isabella of Aragon, the daughter of the Spanish monarchs Ferdinand and Isabella, Portugal's King Manuel I had to promise to expel the Jews from his kingdom too.

Many Jews went to Holland, including an ancestor of mine on my mother's side, Rabbi Chayut, and his family. He eventually moved east, as did many other Jews, and settled in Prague, where he became the chief Rabbi. He was of that particular *Hassidic* (ultra-Orthodox) movement that started in Provence, France, and had a great-grandson, also a Hassidic rabbi, who wrote commentaries on the Hebrew Scriptures.

Eventually, as Jews were expelled from one country after another in Europe, many settled in Poland, where for a time they were welcome. The 1264 Statute of Kalisz created legal protections for Jews that were extended by King Kazimierz Wielki, (also known as Casimir III the Great) in the early fourteenth century. With these protections, Jewish communities in Poland began to thrive. Scholars suggest that by the sixteenth century, 80 percent of all Jews worldwide lived in Poland, where they enjoyed relative autonomy and tolerance, and developed a rich social and cultural life. This included several significant Jewish religious movements, such as the *Hasidim* (a sect of Judaism with an emphasis on mysticism and prayer) and a Jewish reformation movement called the *Haskalah*. Among those Jewish people were my ancestors who moved there. They eventually settled in the area around Krakow, in small towns known as *shtetls* that were typically 100 percent Jewish.

In a memoir that my mother wrote about her family, she describes how her great-grandparents, Leah and Joseph, married when Leah was only thirteen and Joseph seventeen. They were first cousins, which was common back then. They were devoted to each other and their children as well and allowed their daughter, my great-grandmother, to study Hebrew, something that was not permitted for girls in those days (and even today in ultra-orthodox communities).

As was typical in those days, marriages were arranged, and the couple typically did not meet until under the wedding canopy. Mom tells the story of when her own grandmother Atia was engaged to marry, how she accompanied her parents to the home of the boy to meet the family. Her father was a silk merchant, apparently of some prominence. She had to stay in another room by herself but caught a glimpse of her intended husband and was horrified. "He was a big man with a very dark beard and seemingly shifty eyes." Apparently, her parents were not too pleased with him either and the wedding was called off—which was no small matter. The matchmaker was not happy, but soon arranged for another young man whose family lived in another town, who turned out to be her cousin. His name was Elias Langerman. He was a *Tshortkov chassid*, a sect of the Hasidic movement that began in Poland in the 1800s. Elias and Atia eventually had five children; the oldest was my grandmother Sabina.

When Sabina was six years old, the family moved to the outskirts of Krakow into an apartment building in which the Scheidlingers, Hanna and Aaron, lived. Hanna became pregnant, and at seven months, went into labor. Her milk was not yet in and the premature baby was bluish and very tiny. The women neighbors advised her to just let the baby die since Hannah was still young and could have many more children. However, Hanna would not give up her child. She took several layers of flannel and some cotton and rolled the baby up in it and then put him inside her dress. For nourishment, she dipped a cloth in sugar water and let him suck on it till her milk finally came. Of all her children, he was her favorite, and grew up to become a very handsome, intelligent and very social man. That was my grandfather, Gabriel.

Gabriel had dreams of becoming a doctor. He was a good student, and in his first year at the university in 1914, he was drafted into the military to fight for the Kaiser against Russia. His leg was badly wounded in battle, and unable to retreat, he was subsequently captured by the Russians. The Russian doctor wanted to amputate his leg because gangrene had set in but Gabriel refused saying, "I'd rather die with both my legs than live with just one." Fortunately, soon after, there was a prisoner exchange, and he was sent to Vienna to recuperate. While there, he became an assistant to the doctor, going on rounds with him and helping the other wounded soldiers. He was always so proud of this period of his life, as this was as close as he ever came to becoming the doctor of his dreams.

Growing up, when we would visit my grandparents, we would hear this constant lament of my grandfather Gabriel: how he had fought for the Kaiser, that he was a good German, that he was going to be a doctor, and how Hitler had spoiled everything. More on that later.

After the war, Gabriel Scheidlinger and Sabina Langerman became engaged and were married on June 29, 1921. They left Poland and settled in Berlin, and my mom was born a year later on July 27, 1922. Both families, the Scheidlingers and the Langermans, lived in the same building and celebrated Shabbat (Sabbath) together every week. There was always a special meal on Friday night to usher in the Shabbat, and sometimes Grandpa would take Mom to the synagogue on Saturday mornings. Mom was close to her Oma, the German word for grandma, closer than to her own mother. Oma would teach her many things, from the prayers in Hebrew for hand washing and over the bread, to the skill of crochet.

Oma once shared this dramatic story about her grandparents. It was on the night of Passover, while they were celebrating the *seder* or Passover meal that they found the dead body of a Gentile

7

that had been laid by their front door. They were terrified that the police would accuse them of murdering this man. So they washed him and dressed him in the traditional Passover clothing of a white *kittel* (like a priestly robe) and a white *yarmulka* (traditional men's head covering), and they stuck him between two people on the couch. When the police came to the house, they told the police, "Go ahead and search the house; we are not hiding any dead people here," and the police left!

Oma also taught my mother that "When the *Mashiach* (Messiah) comes, we will all go to Palestine. Later in life, Mom would paint, write, knit and crochet, even becoming a needlework instructor as a result of her Oma's influence.

As mentioned, Sabna was the oldest of five children, with two younger sisters and two brothers. They were Zionists. Back then, a Zionist was one who actively worked toward and believed in the restoration of Israel as a homeland for the Jewish people. At a young age, the two sisters and one of the brothers visited what was called Palestine in the 1920s, and eventually settled there and raised their families.

I have been to Israel many times and when I'm there, I visit with some of the cousins on this side of my family. It is from these cousins that I learned about our ancestors, who were rabbis. Their family name in Europe was also Langerman, which means "tall" or "large" man, but when they settled in Israel, they changed their name to Ram, which in Hebrew also means "tall" or "large."

My mom and her sister remained in Berlin with their parents until life took a turn.

CHAPTER 3
RENDEZVOUS IN PARIS: 1937

My grandfather, Gabriel, was an accountant and had a large clientele in Berlin. He was also very active in various religious as well as secular organizations. When the Nazi regime came to power, among their many rules and regulations, was a decree that any meetings of the various clubs and organizations had to be attended and supervised by several Nazis in uniform. As Gabriel was very sociable and outgoing, he always made sure that the Nazis were properly entertained at those functions, particularly at formal balls. Those men then wined and dined and even danced with the pretty, young Jewish girls.

That was how my grandfather became well known to some of the Nazis, to the point where they even offered him a job as a translator. As incoming and outgoing mail with foreign countries was censored, my grandfather, being multilingual, was expected to jump at the chance of working for the Nazis. But he refused when he realized that, for the slightest infraction, the family could very easily end up in the concentration camp.

However, that refusal would eventually turn out not to be so favorable either. As things began to get worse for the Jewish people in Germany, they made plans to escape. My grandfather had a sister who lived with her family in the Bronx, New York, and he was able to secure visas because of their sponsorship to immigrate to the States. At that time, the only way you could come into the United States was through a sponsor.

After four years of waiting to be granted those precious visas to immigrate to the States, my grandparents decided to leave them with most of their personal belongings at a trustworthy neighbor's house. They were going to Krakow, Poland, for a farewell visit with my grandfather's sisters and families. They were then to return to Berlin and stay at a hotel since they had already given up their apartment and sold most of their belongings. They also had more money than they were allowed to take out of Germany, so they anticipated that the return to Berlin after Krakow would be a splash. They seemed to have forgotten how desperate they were to leave Germany and how long it took to get those priceless visas—or perhaps my grandfather was still thinking Hitler's regime was just a passing phase.

However, while they were still in Krakow, my grandparents received an anonymous postcard, warning my grandfather not to return to Germany. Apparently, one of his client's income tax returns did not suit the Nazis and, that client decided to blame my grandfather for the discrepancies.

As soon as they read the postcard, they realized that my grandfather could certainly not return to Berlin. However, the rest of the family was also in danger, as the Nazis would just as easily haul them to the concentration camp in order to get at my grandfather. It was finally decided that only my grandmother, my mother, and mom's sister Gisi would return to Berlin and hope for the best. My grandfather was to go to Switzerland and then, in a roundabout way, finally meet them in Paris, where they would take the train to the port and sail to America.

My grandmother hastily packed a small bag for him, and they planned to meet him at the hotel in Paris as earlier arranged by their travel agent. Then the three of them took the train back to Berlin. They were extremely fearful of crossing the border, expecting the Nazis to be looking out for them.

Fortunately, they made it back to Berlin without trouble. However, instead of returning to their old neighborhood, my grandmother decided to go across town to stay with a cousin, thinking they would be safer there. But the Nazis had already been looking for them at her home, and the cousin was finally persuaded to keep them only for the night as she, too, was shortly leaving Germany. As they were getting ready for bed, there was a person-to-person call from my grandfather to my grandmother. He desperately needed the American immigration visa in order to travel through the various countries to get to Paris. No country was going to risk taking in some refugee.

After some deliberation, they decided for my grandfather to try to get to France the best way he could, as it was certainly too late and too unsafe to mail the visa to him. Further, knowing the Nazis intercepted all foreign calls, they were now in even more jeopardy. My grandmother and my mom never slept that night; they stayed up and listened behind curtained windows for the heavy boot-steps of the Nazis. *Were they going to stop in front of the house? Were they coming for us?*

"What should we do?" my grandmother fearfully asked. "Shall we say good-by now or when they put a gun to our heads?" Mom knew she was trembling. *Actually, a gun to the head was an easy way out at that time, preferable to the unimaginable tortures in the concentration camps*, she thought. Gisi, only eleven at the time, was the only one who slept through the night.

Very early the next morning, they quietly left. They decided to split up just in case they got caught. Gisi was to go with her mother; my mom, who was fifteen, felt that she could fend for herself. My grandmother gave her money to spend as she saw fit: they couldn't take it with them anyway. My grandmother and Gisi were going to Mrs. Bienfelt, the neighbor, who kept their things and was not afraid to hide them.

Mom took a trolley to another part of town where there was a well-known beauty salon, and stopped there to get a perm. Not that she needed it, but it killed some time. Then she took a subway to another section of Berlin to an elegant department store. As it was a Saturday, a busy day, she mingled with the customers, while constantly on the alert and looking over her shoulder.

"All the time I was mortally scared and yet, at times, it felt exhilarating," she recounted. "It felt as if I were in a spy novel playing the heroine."

She bought a few needless items in the store, dawdled, and then ate something somewhere, until it was time to return to the neighbor's house to meet my grandmother and sister. They planned to leave Berlin that night and go to Paris. It was almost two weeks before their sailing date from Le Havre, and they hoped it would give my grandfather enough time to find them.

The neighbor, Mrs. Bienfeld, gave them scarves to cover their heads to partially hide their faces, and called a taxi—someone she knew. They got to the station just in time as the train was ready to pull out. At this point, they were not recognized or stopped. They had a long night and the border crossing to look forward to.

After they got settled in theirseats, my grandmother whispered to my mom, "What are we going to do if they catch us at the border?" There were only two elderly women in their compartment, and they appeared to be asleep. Still, they had learned to speak in whispers, even in their own house, after the Hitler regime took over.

"And, if we get to Paris, should we stay there till Papa comes, or what?" Grandma fretted.

"We'll wait for a few days," mom said, trying to calm her, "until we need to be in Le Havre." That night, my mom became an adult, the mother-figure and decision-maker. My grandmother had always depended heavily on my grandfather. He had to go with them to buy their clothes, shoes, and school supplies; he even had to decide where to spend their vacations. My grandmother never took a trolley or subway by herself; perhaps she preferred to be dependent. But now the responsibility fell on my mom. "I could only hope for wisdom to make the right decisions," she wrote.

It was September of 1937 at the time they were leaving for the States. Paris was hosting the World Fair, and so the town was overbooked. They were not expected at their hotel for another week, so the reservations were not honored. The travel agent dragged them from one hotel to another until they finally found a room in some third class pension. They did not care—they had made it! Physically exhausted and emotionally spent, they needed sleep and food. They would take turns leaving the hotel, fearing that they might miss my grandfather if he was, indeed, lucky enough to get to Paris without the American visa. Mom had four years of French in school, so she now had double duty. She got the food; she made inquiries about train schedules from Paris to Le Havre, while constantly assuring my grandmother everything would be all right—whether she actually believed it or not.

Then it happened. On Thursday morning, they had just gotten up. There was a knock on the door, and there was my grandfather! Their joy was overwhelming! It was almost unbelievable! They were all finally together and safe. My grandfather had already been in Paris for several days but was unable to get any information regarding their whereabouts. With the World Fair in town, Paris was just too busy—too many people—to be concerned about one lone traveler.

"How did you get here from Poland?" they asked. He described how he had called the American consulate in Warsaw to verify that he had visas to come to the States. The consulate there got in touch with the other consulates in Austria and Italy to give him the permits to pass through. That is how he had made it! Because there were no rooms available in Paris, he had slept in a bathtub and somewhere on a floor. He had been in Paris three days before he came knocking on their door.

Obviously, they were overjoyed, and felt an incredible sense of freedom after living in fear of their lives for the past four years under Hitler. They'd seen friends disappear; they too were harassed and assaulted on the streets, and they knew about the "labor camps" that Jews were being taken to. The fear that they must have experienced in those days in Berlin under Hitler, and especially in those latter days separated from grandpa, must have been unimaginable. So much is passed from generation to generation; even that fear would be carried forward and play a big role through the generations to come—and into my life as well.

And now a new problem cropped up. That very night was *Yom Kippur*, the Day of Atonement, the evening of the holiest day of the Jewish calendar. They, of course, were very eager to find a synagogue to attend service. What could be more appropriate than to thank God for the blessings they had received, to be out of harm's way and united as a family!

And so, together, they left the hotel in great spirits, not knowing which way would take them to a synagogue. Then suddenly my grandfather stopped to speak to someone in a dark doorway. A small man with a pronounced limp appeared and my grandfather motioned for them to follow. They walked for many blocks, making left and right turns, in and out of different streets. Finally, the man said something to my grandfather, and they all stopped. My grandfather turned to the rest of the family to repeat the information the man had given him. They were just a couple of blocks from a synagogue. When he turned back to thank the man, the man was gone! They looked in all directions, but there was not a trace of him. Just vanished into thin air! They just stood there, dumbfounded. How did that limping man disappear so fast?

My grandfather slowly shook his head in disbelief, then turned to his family and solemnly said, "We all need to remember this moment. That cripple must be an angel sent by God to direct us to the temple. And now we'll offer special prayers for the miracles

14

of these last few days." Overwhelmed, they walked in silence to the synagogue.

The next day, they set sail on the S.S. Paris for the United States. Mom relates how excited they were to finally be on the ship. They were all dressed in their finest clothes. She remembers how Grandpa was all dressed up in his best attire, when promptly at 4:00 p.m. as the ship was leaving the port, a woman of the family they were traveling with threw up all over his new suit! One by one, they all got sick with the exception of my mom and a boy from the other family because in September the Atlantic can be rough. So the two of them got to enjoy all the food that was meant for the two families!

On their arrival in New York, the family settled in the South Bronx. My grandfather's sister and her husband, the ones who sponsored the family to the U.S., owned a paint store. My grand-father went to work for his brother-in-law as a painter since he couldn't work as an accountant due to the language barrier.

At that time, my mom was fifteen years old and had started high school. She and her sister subsequently heard about a Viennese club, the Maccabees, a swim and social club that would meet socially on Wednesdays and swim on Sunday. So on a Wednesday, Mom and her sister went. They were sitting on a couch and there were two guys coming up the walkway. One was blonde and blue eyed, the other had dark hair and dark eyes. Both were very good looking. She said to her sister, "That guy is for me!" Her sister thought it was the dark-haired guy because she liked him, but my mom meant the blonde guy. They were brothers: the blonde guy was Joe, and the dark guy was Walter. Joe and Lilly were married on March 3, 1941. Dad was twenty-two and mom was eighteen.

CHAPTER 4

THE STEIGER AFFAIR

The family history on my dad's side of the family contains some colorful stories of survival in the face of hardship and difficulty that are tremendously inspiring. One of those stories came to be known as "The Steiger Affair," and became famous in Europe at the time.

The Steiger event came about twenty years after another famous event called the "Dreyfus Affair." The Dreyfus affair was a case of wrongful accusation against a Jewish army captain in France.It triggered a national crisis over antisemitism in France in the late 19th century and had wide international repercussions.

Briefly, Alfred Dreyfus was a 36-year-old Jewish French army captain, from the Alsace region of France which was at the time occupied by Germany. He was accused of passing secret information on new artillery equipment to the German military attaché. Despite the lack of evidence, he was convicted of treason on December 22, 1894, and sentenced to life imprisonment as well as publicly stripped of his rank.[1]

Lieutenant Colonel Georges Picquart, head of the intelligence services, reinvestigating the case discovered in 1896 that the handwriting on the incriminating message was that of another officer,

---

1   Alfred Dreyfus was found guilty of espionage in a kangaroo court in late 19th century France (Public domain/Wikimedia commons)

Ferdinand Walsin Esterhazy. When he presented the evidence to the general staff of the French army, they refused to admit there had been a mistake. Esterhazy was court-martialed and acquitted after a farce of a trial in 1898; he then moved to England.

In June 1899, Dreyfus was brought back to France for a second trial and found guilty. After many twists and turns, the high court of appeal overturned the original verdict, thus exonerating Dreyfus. He was reinstated with the rank of major. He served during World War I and died in 1935, aged 76, but there was general indifference to his passing.

The young Hungarian Jewish journalist, Theodor Herzl, closely followed the Dreyfus affair, and was disgusted by the antisemitism it revealed. The man who became regarded as the "Father of Zionism" later said that the Dreyfus affair had motivated his belief that Jews should move out of Europe and set up their own state instead.

OUR STEIGER COUSINS

This brings to mind a similar case that occurred some twenty years later regarding Stanislaw Steiger, a cousin of my grandmother's, who lived in Lvov, Poland. Historically, Lvov (also known as Lemberg for a time) was part of Ukraine, when Poland invaded the western part of Ukraine including Lvov in 1919, and subsequently annexed it. While it was technically part of Poland, it was clearly Ukrainian historically and culturally. This brought tremendous tension as there were groups agitating to overthrow Polish rule in the area. In addition, Lvov had a large Jewish community, consisting of socialists or communists, and some Zionists.

Stanislaw Steiger was then a twenty-four-year-old law student in Lvov while working at a local law firm. He took no interest in politics and belonged only to a Zionist student organization, Maccabea. On September 5, 1924, the President of the Polish

Republic, Stanislaw Wojciechowski was in Lvov for the opening of the IV Eastern Trade Fair. As his procession passed through the main square in the city, a bomb was thrown from the crowd at his open carriage. It did not explode, and nobody was hurt. However, the police, acting on information given by a woman, Maria Pasternak, arrested our cousin, Stanislaw Steiger, for the attempt on the president's life. Word got out pretty quickly that a Jewish student had attempted to kill the president and antisemitic excesses broke out in various parts of the city. The entire Jewish community in Poland found itself "indicted and imperiled."

This incident went far beyond the sphere of Polish-Jewish relations, into Polish-Ukrainian relations, and even the International Polish-German conflict. Germany at the time supported the Ukrainian nationalist effort to reclaim the western portion of its territory from Poland.

Under the Polish judicial system at the time, Steiger faced two trials. The first was called a "Summary trial" which took place ten days after the attempted assassination. If after hearing the evidence all four judges agreed on his guilt, he would be hung without any further proceedings. The only witness, Maria Pasternak, reaffirmed her previous account that it was Steiger that threw the bomb. Steiger pleaded not guilty. When asked why he ran away, he replied, "Either bombs or flowers are thrown at a president, and the parcel thrown did not look like flowers." He had been scared and bolted like others in the crowd. Three judges were for conviction, one against, so Steiger was spared. Now the issue would go to a jury trial. However, it began a firestorm of antisemitism led by the Catholic press and the right wing.

Ironically, a member of the Ukrainian resistance, Teofil Olszanski was detained two weeks after the attempt on the president for illegally crossing the Polish-German border. He was seeking asylum in Berlin and told his interrogators that he was the perpetrator of the attack on the Polish president. However, his case remained secret for almost a year, and his testimony was discredited by the prosecution who obviously were only looking to Steiger as the culprit.

The Steiger trial lasted from October 11 until December 18, 1925. The jury was selected by drawing lots behind closed doors. Not a single Jew or Ukrainian, the two groups that constituted a majority of the population of Lvov, sat on the panel of jurors.

In spite of the defense obtaining evidence of UMO (Ukraine Military Organization) responsibility including Olszanski's confession, albeit from Germany, the prosecution was relentless in pursuing a conviction against Steiger. It later came out that the political police of Lvov had withheld exculpatory evidence that would prove his innocence. "The Steiger Affair," as it became known, was increasingly assuming the proportions of a political scandal throughout eastern Europe and Germany, arousing deep-rooted antisemitism, with reactions from socialists, communists, and Ukrainian nationalists alike.

The verdict was returned ten weeks after the trial had started. Despite the obvious bias of the presiding judge in trying to influence the jury against Steiger, the jury returned a verdict of not guilty, by a vote of 8-4. After fifteen months of being incarcerated, with physical and emotional suffering, Stanislaw Steiger was released from prison. Crowds of Jews lined the streets to cheer him, along with the defense lawyers and the jurors. The Steiger affair shored up the political strife that was tearing the country apart and the corruption and antisemitism prevalent in the police and judicial system.

The acquittal gave rise to violent antisemitic disturbances in Lvov. A crowd of several thousand people, mostly students, loudly cheered Maria Pasternak, the lone witness against Steiger, then proceeded toward Steiger's home and the homes of the defense lawyers and jurors, where they violently demonstrated and smashed windows. Jews were held up and beaten in the streets. A café frequented by Jews was destroyed.

Under these conditions, Steiger left Lvov for Warsaw and went abroad. He completed his law studies and sometime later returned to Poland. Shortly before the war he lived in another city in Poland, Bedzin, where he ran a law firm. During the Nazi occupation he was killed along with most Polish Jews.[2]

ANOTHER STEIGER STORY

Another Steiger cousin, Josef Ulrich, rose to fame (within the family) in Nazi-occupied Poland. Josef's mother was a cousin of Stanislaw as well as my grandmother. Josef was born in 1922 and the family stayed in Lvov till nearly the end of World War II. His story is documented in the Shoah project in an interview he gave in 1997. In his story, he recounts the events leading up to the German invasion of Poland on September 1, 1939.

At the time, because Germany and Russia had a pact, first Russia had invaded from the east. At first it seemed like a good thing that Russia had come in and instituted Communism. Very quickly, however, there were food shortages and the private businesses, including the one owned by Josef's father were nationalized. Because Josef did not look that Jewish, he was able to blend in and finish school, with his Marxist inclinations.

Anti-semitism, which was always present in Polish society, had become widespread by now, and there were boycotts of Jewish merchants. When the German-Russian pact was dissolved by Germany, the Nazis could now invade and take over that area in 1941. Under Russian occupation, life was somewhat normal, but all that changed when the Germans came in.

---

2   http://www.lamoth.info/?p=collections/findingaid&id=132&q=&rootcontentid
=14354
https://ukrainianjewishencounter.org/en/a-ukrainian-bomb-a-polish-target-a
-jewish-victim/

Now the Jewish people in Lvov had to wear armbands with a "J" on it. In August 1942 there was a raid that lasted over two weeks. During that time over 40,000 Jews were rounded up and taken to Auschwitz, including his mother and his thirteen-year-old sister. Josef was spared and continued to live in Lvov with his father but was forced to give up their apartment and they moved in with his father's business partner.

Due to the kindness of a German man that befriended Josef, he was able to get a job with a supply organization called TODT that belonged to the *Wehrmacht* (the German army). It was a section of the civil and military engineering organization that transported supplies back and "conquered goods" back and forth from Russia to Germany via train. The Germans would bring these goods from the Russian side up to the Lvov train station and then have them shipped from there on the narrower-gauged tracks to Germany. The goods had to be stored temporarily in a warehouse.

Josef along with nine other men worked there *schlepping* or hauling huge loads every day. They were able to survive by skimming goods and helping their friends. Among the items that were being shipped were uniforms of dead German officers. They found that they could save their lives by taking on forged German identities and supplying the forms and permits that were needed to escape to the eastern front. So Josef started to put away—a belt here, a pair of trousers there, a cap here—and, slowly but surely, they had assembled uniforms, not complete but more a mix between SS and military uniforms. Everyone who worked on the Eastern front for the Germans had to wear a yellow armband that said "Eastern Front." According to Josef's testimony, there was so much going on that it didn't matter, as long as you had the yellow armband and looked somewhat professional.

On January 5 1943, the Germans staged a raid on Josef's ghetto. Everyone was ordered outside. However, early that morning Josef had a dream about his mother, and she warned him not to go with the others but leave the ghetto a different way. Around 4.00 that same morning, people were ordered to come outside. Based on the dream, he gathered his nine coworkers and they climbed over the ghetto wall in another location. They were shot at but, because it was still dark, they managed to escape. Many of the inhabitants of the ghetto were shot that night. The next day Josef and company showed up for work as if nothing had happened.

Subsequently, Josef along with a group of friends, were able to escape Poland using their forged papers and the stolen uniforms of dead German officers obtained from the transport trains. They eventually made their way to Romania. Josef survived the war, and settled in Vienna, where he lived until his death in the early 2000s.

The mug shot of Stanislaw Steiger from a Polish newspaper circa September 5, 1924.

CHAPTER 5
LIFE IN PRE-WAR VIENNA

On my mantelpiece is a framed photo of a family reunion in Poland taken in 1921 of some members of the Steiger family. It was given to me by my Uncle Walter a few years ago. When I asked him about the people in that picture, who were on vacation at this well-known resort town of Otwack, he simply said that they were all killed in the Holocaust.

In the late 1800s, Otwack grew as a resort and health spa that was frequented by well-off Jewish people. People would come at various times of the year for vacations, spa and health reasons, particularly tuberculosis treatment. 75 percent of the population were Jewish and the rest Christian; they apparently got along well together. They even had a town charter that spelled out how many Jews and how many Christians would sit on the town council.

Then came World War II with the invasion of Poland in September 1939. The town of Otwack was attacked by the Nazis, and most of the Jewish inhabitants were eventually rounded up and murdered. Some Jewish children were given to nuns, who hid them until after the war, and thus they survived. But, largely, the town was destroyed, and nearly all of the Jewish population either died of starvation or were shipped off to the death camps.

My paternal grandfather, Leo, grew up in Poland. His father's name was actually Andacht, and his mother was a Brawer. But because at that time only marriages that were performed in the

Catholic church were recognized—not those performed by a rabbi—his parents had to give him his mother's name, Brawer. A small comment, but I would much rather be a Brawer than an Andacht!

FROM LVOV TO VIENNA

Pre-war Vienna was a flourishing center of Jewish life. Jews had been welcomed into Austria since the Hapsburg statute was enacted in 1890. At that time, the Jewish population in Vienna was 160,000, which was roughly ten percent of the population. Jewish people were involved in all of the cultural, business, and political life of the city. Altogether, there were an estimated 440 synagogues, and over fifty prayer houses. There was a Jewish Museum, Jewish libraries, schools, hospitals, and medical clinics, orphanages, sports clubs, Yiddish theaters, kosher kitchens, Zionist organizations, political associations, newspapers and journals, and many charitable foundations, clubs, and associations, most notably, the Jewish World War I Veterans Association.

My grandfather, Leo, who fought for the Kaiser in World War I, moved the family from Poland to Vienna shortly after the war. My dad, Joseph, was born in what was then called Lemburg in Poland in 1918, now called Lvov and part of Ukraine. Leo was a successful furrier in Vienna and had his own business. Dad was the oldest of three children; his siblings, Walter and Anita, were born in Vienna.

As a thriving cultural center in Europe, Vienna was home to many famous composers such as Mozart, Shubert, and Strauss. Music pervaded the air. My dad, Joseph, or Yoshi, as he was affectionately called in Yiddish, grew up immersed in this music, taking piano lessons as a child.

24

THE FAMOUS *HAKOAH*

In Vienna at the time, there were a number of sports clubs. Unfortunately, in most cases, Jews were not allowed to join. So we did what we always did when doors were closed: we created our own. In this case, it was a Jewish sports club called *Hakoah*, which is Hebrew for "the strength." There were teams formed for soccer, fencing, field hockey, track and field, wrestling, water polo, and swimming. Tours and competitions were held throughout Europe, which drew widespread support among the Jewish communities. Their teams competed against local teams in cities such as London and New York. At its pre-WW II peak, the club had over 8,000 members.

However, by the 1930s, Hakoah Vienna was on the receiving end of hatred stirred up by Hitler and had to travel to matches with their wrestlers as bodyguards. Three days after the *Anschluss*, German for "union," the shared club base of Hakoah Sports Club, Hakoah Tourism and Ski Club, and the Hakoah Swimming Club at the Viennese Cafe Atlashof, were shut down, with the club assets and stadium seized.

Dad and Uncle Walter had become members of the Hakoah Sports Club as swimmers and water polo players. My dad's commitment to the sport of swimming would have an impact and influence on our family and my life for years thereafter, even until today. The Hakoah sports club became very famous and produced several Olympic athletes, including a female swimmer, Judith Deutsch, who was an Austrian national champion. Her story, along with that of other Hakoah swimmers and athletes, is beautifully portrayed in the recent documentary *Watermarks*. Because she chose not to attend the 1936 Olympics in Berlin in protest against Hitler, she was stripped of her Austrian championship title, although it was symbolically restored to her in 2004.

The coach of the swimming team was a man by the name of Zsigo Werthheimer. He was loved by all, and had a profound impact not only on coaching, but on inspiring the athletes in all areas. He was also instrumental in helping many of the athletes escape when the Nazis came into Austria in 1938. He was also to be instrumental in our lives in the United States a few years later.

While the tide of antisemitism was rising in Austria in the 1930s, it wasn't until March 12, 1938 that things started to change drastically for the Austrian Jewish community. That was the day of the Anschluss when the Nazi army marched into Vienna. As a result, the anti-Jewish laws that had been decreed by Hitler in Germany now extended to the Jewish community in Austria. Properties and assets of Jewish businesses were seized or destroyed, and there were widespread demonstrations of violence and persecution against the Jewish people. Sadly, the vast majority of Austrian citizens welcomed the annexation into Germany. Shortly after the Anschluss, the Nazis shut down the Hakoah Club and seized its assets, including its stadium and training facilities.

ESCAPE FROM VIENNA

A year before the German annexation of Austria, my dad was swimming and playing water polo in Hakoah, when he was tipped off by the daughter of a Swiss diplomat he was dating that he was in danger of being picked up by the authorities. (My dad was also involved in the Zionist movement.) In addition, conditions for Jews were deteriorating, and mandatory conscription was put into effect. Joe was nineteen at the time, and he was able to get on a ship from Europe to South America. He was able to secure a visa through his cousins, the Steigers, who had emigrated to Uruguay years earlier.

The rest of the Brawer family were still in Vienna operating the fur business. At some point when the Nazis were seizing Jewish assets, they "legally" took over the fur store of my grandfather's. Fortunately, my grandparents, and my uncle Walter and aunt Anita were able to get out in August of 1938 and join my dad in Uruguay.

After getting settled in Montevideo, my grandfather, my dad, and uncle Walter crossed the river into Buenos Aires and went into the fur business there. Unfortunately, due to the wartime situation, they did not do well, and the business closed. Not long after, my dad managed to get a visa to come to the States, leaving from Buenos Aires on the SS Brazil on February 14, 1940, and arriving in New York on March 4. The rest of the family followed soon after, and they all settled in New York.

Sometime later that year, Joe and Lilly met at a German Jewish immigrants' social club and were married on March 3, 1940. Three days later, Dad enlisted in the army. We believe that having enlisted enabled him to obtain a fast track to U.S. citizenship. His brother Walter enlisted in February 1943. Joe was stationed at Ft. Jackson, South Carolina, where my brother Ron was born on February 20, 1943.

I remember my parents telling me that because German was their first language, they typically spoke it. But the neighbors did not like it because they associated it with Nazi Germany. The last thing people wanted to hear was the German language, and my parents were even suspected of being spies.

THE RITCHIE BOYS

Growing up, I only knew that my dad had been a "translator" for German POWs in Germany. After all, that made sense since he was fluent in the language and knew the culture. But I never asked him the questions that I would like to ask him now, about his experiences in the war. As was typical of that generation, they did not really want to talk about the horrors of what they may have gone through during that time.

But I recently read a book about a unit established during the war consisting of Jewish German and Austrian young men that were trained in intelligence gathering and interrogation. There was a training camp in Maryland called Camp Ritchie. It was the first time in the history of warfare that natives of the enemy country were trained to fight against their home countries. In this case, these men were eager because many of them had left their family behind who were either being persecuted or killed by the Nazis, and they were motivated to help win the war. Those that were trained in Camp Ritchie were dispersed throughout Europe into combat units to interrogate both, captured Nazi soldiers as well as civilians. They were nicknamed "the Ritchie boys."

I recently found out that my dad was a Ritchie boy too. He had been at Camp Ritchie for six weeks in 1944 and was then assigned to a combat unit that saw action in Czechoslovakia toward the end of the war. He was slightly injured when a bullet grazed his thumb while he was holding a pistol, for which he received a purple heart. I remember as a boy thinking that it was kind of a joke, that dad was "wounded" in the war—his finger got nicked.

Dad's brother, my Uncle Walter, was four years younger than dad and also enlisted in February1943. Both he and my dad, besides being swimmers, were also skiers. As a result, Uncle Walter joined the 10th Mountain Division of the Army. They trained to fight with skis in the mountains of Colorado and then fought in Northern Italy in the famous battle of Riva Ridge, which was a key turning point in the allies' fight to liberate Italy. He was seriously wounded in that battle—more than a nicked finger. Years later, when we were living in Colorado, Uncle Walter attended a re-union of the 10th Mountain Division of WWII and invited us to join them for a ski in the Colorado mountains and to attend a reunion banquet which was a memorable experience.

CHAPTER 6
NOT-SO HUMBLE BEGINNINGS

When I was younger, I did not have the same level of interest in knowing the family stories that I came to know later. If I had, I would have asked both my mom and dad, and my grandparents more questions about what it was like in Nazi Germany. *At what point did you know it was time to leave? What were the emotions you felt as you left everything for an unknown future? What was it like, Dad, to go back to Germany, and risk your life against those who were the source of the disruption in your life?*

If I could go back and ask the earlier family members similar questions, what kind of answers would I get? *What was it like for the Chayut family to have to up and leave Portugal, then later settle in Prague, where Yitzhak rose to prominence to be chief Rabbi? What about being falsely accused of an attempted assassination of the President of Poland, sitting in jail for fifteen months without knowing your fate, and being the center of controversy and international tension? What about barely surviving through the Holocaust in the same city where the famous trial took place?*

These stories carry such emotional weight for me now. I see some similarities in all the stories, of the character and commitment of my family members. In most cases, they were confronted with circumstances beyond their control, and were often life threatening. They responded with courage, intelligence, and

29

commitment to future generations. In some cases, it was about survival and doing whatever was necessary. Had they not taken those risks and responded with courage and action, I and my children would not be here today. I am grateful for their example of overcoming in the face of adversity and hardship, and for their perseverance and determination to live.

But, most of all, I am grateful to the One who protected and preserved them so I could live the life that I have. I have not faced any of the challenges that they faced. However, I do see some characteristics in common as I reflect on my life—in some cases, the pioneering spirit and risk-taking, among other things.

After the war, my parents moved to a Manhattan apartment and eventually were able to purchase a house in Valley Stream, Long Island. At that time, my brother Ron was seven, and then I came along on April 20, 1950. Ironically, I was born on Hitler's birthday. I am sure my parents knew, especially my mom, having lived under Hitler for four years, where his birthday was practically a national holiday. Ironically, today is also almost a national holiday here, but for way other reasons, which I came to find out about more recently.

Well, we lived in Long Island until I was seven years old. For me, those early years in Long Island were great. I remember being able to walk down the street and visit friends, play outside, and ride bikes. It was like living in the country. The extended family used to come visit, Uncle Walter and his wife Hannah, and my Dad's younger sister, Anita, and her husband, Leon. One Sunday, Uncle Leon and Aunt Anita came and surprised us with a puppy, a black cocker spaniel. We named her Princess. She was with us only a short time, and one day she was gone. Mom and Dad said that she got sick, and they had to put her down. I always wondered if they just gave her away and didn't tell us. I do not think that they were into having a dog. That was a sad moment.

A sadder moment happened not too long after. My dad decided to move us into the city, to Manhattan. Why? I loved it here in

Valley Stream! When we moved to Long Island, my dad had opened a fur store in a nearby town to carry on the family business. My grandfather and Uncle Walter had their business in the NY garment center, but my dad wanted to go on his own. However, the business failed.

Meanwhile, Dad's former coach, Zsigo Werthheimer, from Hakoah, Vienna, had rented a pool in the basement of the Hotel Paris on West End Avenue in the upper Westside of Manhattan. He started a swim club and school there and offered my dad a job, which he took. So rather than commuting from Long Island into the city like many did, he wanted to live near the business. So he moved us into an apartment on 98th Street and Broadway, just three blocks from the pool. I was devastated because I loved my life in Valley Stream. My brother, on the other hand, who was now fourteen, was glad because now that he was in the city, he had the freedom to go out and explore.

While I had attended kindergarten in Valley Stream, now it was time for real school, to start 1st grade. What kind of school was I going to go to? My parents agreed that I should go to a *yeshiva*, a Jewish day school. We weren't particularly religious at that time, but because both Mom and Dad had experienced such incredible antisemitism growing up in Germany and Austria, and because it was only twelve years after the Holocaust, they feared the same discrimination might exist in the public schools.

So, we looked around and settled on a small school, Beth Hillel. It was just starting and was connected to a synagogue in our neighborhood on the upper west side, Ohev Zedek. I was there from 1st to 3rd grade; that's as far as the school went at that time. In a school like that, you learn Hebrew, Jewish history, Torah, and Jewish music and songs in addition to the usual subjects, English, math, and so on. We also started to attend the synagogue service every Shabbat morning and were involved in the congregation. Later, I was even in the choir.

31

Every morning I would walk the five or six blocks to school. We're talking NYC in the late 1950s. Who would send their 1st or 2nd grader to walk by themselves today? Things sure have changed. On the next street from where we lived, there were a couple of large Catholic churches. My parents, out of fear of the antisemitism perpetrated by those who called themselves Christians or Catholics that they grew up with, told us to cross the street rather than walk in front of the church. I would do one more thing before crossing: I would spit on the ground in front of the church. After all, it was these Christians who were responsible for the deaths of so many friends and family members along with millions of other Jews. It was all fresh in our minds at that time and has had a huge impact on the minds of Jews for generations since.

During this time, because my dad worked at the swim club, I learned to swim at a young age and started to complete. For that, I am very grateful, as learning to swim at a young age was not only the continuation of a family tradition that started with Dad's experience in Hakoah, and having a great time in competitions through high school, but it has also helped me to stay healthy even now into my 70s.

Not too long after moving into NYC, and living in the apartment, several things began to occur. For one, I started getting fat. I went through the only period of my life where I was chubby, the result of city living. But, more importantly, my parents began to fight more and more, and it was not pretty. I remember one time the argument was so bad that I just went into the room I shared with my brother and cried. He told me at that moment that Mom and Dad were most likely going to separate, or divorce, and who did I want to live with? This was so painful for me. Going to a traditional Jewish school, and being part of an Orthodox synagogue, divorce was unheard of back then generally but especially in the Jewish world.

So, sure enough, not too long after, they sat us down and announced that they would be separating. I was eleven years old at the time, and now I was going to a larger school, Ramaz, also a yeshiva. This was devastating to me, and a source of shame and fear that set me up for many years to come.

By attending an Orthodox school, and still being part of the synagogue where I went until the 3rd grade, the assumption and expectation were that you would be living as Orthodox Jews. What did that mean? Well, some of the main things were that you are not supposed to drive on Shabbat, you are supposed to keep kosher, which not only meant the foods we ate but also having two sets of dishes and silverware, one for meat and one for dairy. Then on Passover, you must use two other sets of dishes and silverware. But, when no one was looking, we violated those things. We would drive on Shabbat but pretend that we were walking everywhere, especially to synagogue. We kept kosher at home, but on Saturday nights we would go to the Chinese restaurant and order shrimp and lobster!

So, it was very confusing. Now, with the separation and divorce added to it, there began to be a lot of shame in me. Outwardly, we were this nice religious family, me in the yeshiva and us attending synagogue every Shabbat, but in the house there was turmoil and, on the side, we violated Shabbat by driving and eating unclean foods.

My dad moved out and got his own apartment a few blocks away. I clearly remember the day he moved out with a suitcase in hand. It changed my life forever, although it did stop the daily fighting and conflicts. And then there was the day, not too long after that, when my brother got on a bus to go off to college. I know that he was really glad to get away. I was heartbroken. Ron was my protector, and I looked up to him a great deal. There was this scene, which I clearly remember. We were at the bus station, Mom and Dad, and my grandparents on mom's side. Dad had borrowed money earlier on from my grandfather to help buy the house in Long Island. Now, some years later, they were divorced; but he still owed my grandfather money.

So there was this big argument that started as the bus was pulling away. I was just standing there as it got louder. I remember trying to back away because I was so embarrassed. My world began to crumble even more; there was my protector leaving, and now my parents and grandparents, those close to me, were in a heated argument. It was many years later that I realized how much the divorce and all the fighting and arguing had affected me, how much shame I carried, and how much healing I needed.

So life continues, and I adjust to living with just my mom, and spending weekends with my dad. Living with Mom was difficult. She was very critical, always complaining about Dad and money. After school, I would attend an after-school day camp called Children's Colony. We would play games, go ice skating, and do sports, which was lots of fun. There was also the summer camp in Connecticut that I looked forward to going to every year to get away from the city and the situation at home.

Summer camp was great. It was on a big lake. We did boating, swimming, water skiing, campfires, baseball, basketball, and more. It was co-ed, so we also had square dancing and social activities, which were enjoyable as I was now interested in girls. My brother worked for a couple of years as a lifeguard. I remember one time some older kids were bullying me, and I went to him, and he "took care of it." It never happened again.

I remember that before we went to summer camp, there was always a checklist. We had to make sure we had the right clothing, shoes, bathing suits, stationery and postcards for writing home. One day, Mom sent me to the stationery store with two dollars to buy paper and envelopes. I found a nice box that had both stationery and envelopes all together. When I came home, Mom was angry that I had spent too much money, and that I had to go back to the store, return the box, and just buy a pad of paper and a pack of envelopes, which was cheaper. It was extremely embarrassing and shameful.

That incident was something that I had totally forgotten about, until many years later, when Gloria and I were on one of our trips to Israel and we were shopping. She was looking for something specific, and every time she saw something, I would say, "Let's keep looking; I'm sure we can find it cheaper." Then, all of a sudden the memory of what happened with Mom and the stationery came flooding back, and I realized where some of my attitudes about money came from. On the one hand, my mom was always complaining about money and how irresponsible my dad was; on the other, my dad was a spender and seemed to have a less stressful attitude toward money.

That moment in Israel came as an incredible revelation, and from that moment on, my attitude toward money changed. I felt a sense of healing from the hurt of that event that had affected me for so many years. As a believer in God, it is easy to say, "He will supply all of my needs," but it is another thing to really believe and act upon it.

I was still in the yeshiva, and on weekends with dad we would have Shabbat dinner (Friday nights) at my grandparents, go to synagogue on Shabbat, and then do something afterwards, like visiting the other relatives. There was my Aunt Anita, Dad's sister, and her husband, Leon Lobel, and their three children, Linda, Evan and Wendy, my cousins. There was my Uncle Walter, Dad's brother, and his wife, Hannah, and their two children, Vivian and Gary. It was always fun to be with the cousins, especially the Lobels. They lived in a nice house out in Long Island. Over the years, I became very close to them, especially my Uncle Leon.

When the Brawers left Vienna, Anita was only five years old. When they got to NY after the time in Uruguay, they settled in an apartment on the upper west side. A few years later, when Anita was around eighteen, her parents sent her out to shop at the local kosher butcher, Lobels Meats. Working there was the son of the owner, Leon. They fell in love and married a year later. They had a beautiful marriage and loved each other deeply. For me, having seen my parents fight and ultimately split up, I felt very safe with them and looked forward to any time that we would be together. That relationship would last until their untimely deaths in 2006 (Leon) and 2012 (Anita). They had a winter home in Boca, and when we moved down to Boca in 1990, we would be with them often. They loved our children and became like grandparents to them.

Curiously, when I was about eleven or twelve years old, I was once with Uncle Leon, and he said to me, "You are going to be a rabbi one day!"

My response was, "No way!" That was the furthest thing from my mind at that time. But here I am, a Rabbi for over thirty years. Uncle Leon and I continued to have a great relationship until he passed away. He respected what we believed, even if he didn't necessarily understand or agree with it. Aunt Anita was a different story; she was always gracious and kind, but not interested in the reality of our faith. More about that later.

During the period that my parents were getting divorced, I started to act out in school and often got into trouble. I was fighting with other boys, which resulted in my getting detention on a couple of occasions. The elementary school went up to the 6th grade, and students in that grade were chosen to be part of the "service squad." These were the "good" kids that would be given the responsibility of keeping order among the others. The only catch was that if you had been in detention at any time, you would be disqualified. I knew that I would not qualify to be on this "squad" due to my misbehavior. However, Mrs. Basin, the teacher in charge, evidently saw something different. One day she asked to see me, and to my amazement, presented to me the badge for the captain of the squad.

"Me?" I asked.

"Yes, you can do it," was her reply. In picking me, she changed the direction of my life, and I began to straighten up with this new found leadership.

However, my level of shame at home continued to increase as my mom met another man that she would soon marry—a non-Jew. His name was Rubin. He was a nice guy, but he was Puerto Rican and dark skinned. This created a huge problem in the family, mostly with mom's parents and her sister Gisi (short for Giselle), whom she never really got along with. Gisi herself had married a wanna-be opera singer named Leon Wolk. However, he didn't make it as an opera singer, so he became a cantor, and they began to live as Orthodox Jews. This at least was acceptable to the family.

I was still in the yeshiva, still trying to keep up the façade of being religious. But it was getting harder. I immersed myself in my studies, and while I got along with Rubin and it seemed like they were happy together, it was still a source of embarrassment and shame. It was worse when I went to visit my grandparents. My grandmother would harp on how bad it was that my mother had done this and shamed the family by marrying a Gentile. Things were about to get more interesting though.

CHAPTER 7
GRADUATING OUT OF JUDAISM

Like all good Jewish boys, I had my *Bar Mitzvah* when I was thirteen. This is a ceremony that signifies that a Jewish boy has attained the age of religious duty and responsibility. Because I attended an orthodox yeshiva, I could read and understand the Torah in Hebrew, as well as know how to chant the ritual readings, called the *trope*, or cantillations from the Torah scroll.

In the synagogue we attended, it was customary for the Bar Mitzvah boy to read and chant the whole Torah portion. What does that entail? The Torah (the five books of Moses) is divided into 54 portions. Each portion is read in sequence every week on Shabbat in the synagogues. The cycle is universal, meaning that any synagogue in the world is reading the same portion on any given week. For Bar Mitzvahs, the Torah portion is assigned based on your birth date according to the Hebrew calendar, which follows the moon cycles.

Generally, preparation begins a whole year before the actual Bar Mitzvah, and you train with one of the rabbis in the congregation. Each Torah portion is usually around three chapters long. In my synagogue, it was expected that you would learn to chant the whole portion. The Torah scroll does not have punctuation or vowels in the Hebrew, so it's not just reading it. One had to learn where the sentences end, the pronunciation of all the words without vowels, and the melody to chant. Looking back, it is hard to imagine actually learning all this. But somehow, I was able to pull it off.

However, the most difficult part of my Bar Mitzvah happened after the service. Generally, the family has a party, either after the service or later in the evening. With divorced parents, this was difficult. My mom would have a party for a few friends at our apartment after service, and my dad would throw a big shindig at a hotel that evening.

More embarrassment for me!

It was not too long after my Bar Mitzvah that I stopped going to the synagogue altogether. After I finished 8th grade in the yeshiva, I was done. I had applied to Bronx High School of Science, which was a public school, but specialized. That meant you needed to qualify to get in. Initially, I did not get accepted, but by God's grace, another really smart student from our school, who had been accepted, decided to go to a private school. This left an opening, so I was accepted.

That was my ticket out of the religious world. I graduated, not only from 8th grade, but also from Judaism. I stopped going to synagogue, and wasn't concerned about kosher, keeping Shabbat or any other religious practices.

That summer, 1964, I accompanied my mom on a visit to my grandparents in Israel. A couple of years prior, my grandmother said she was missing her siblings terribly, and convinced my grandfather to move to Israel to be close to them. She had two sisters and a brother, and they each had their own families as well. We spent that summer traveling around Israel, just Mom and I, meeting and spending time with all the cousins. It was a very special time. That summer my brother traveled through Europe and joined us for a couple of weeks in Israel.

With my eight years in yeshiva, I spoke decent Hebrew. We always had a connection with the Land. I remember in the 1950s how we used to send care packages to the family in Israel. The country was still in its infancy, and many were struggling for survival. There were also regular appeals at the synagogue for the sale of Israeli bonds. My mom, the firstborn of her mom, who was also the firstborn, was the oldest of all her cousins. The two youngest, Menachem and Yossi, were the sons of my grandmother's youngest brother. They were closer to my age than to my mother's. In recent years, when we go to Israel, we often connect with them. The rest of that generation has since passed on.

A TALE OF TWO BACHELORS

My stepfather, Rubin, was a pharmacist working for Warner Lambert (now owned by Pfizer). Shortly after, Warner Lambert acquired a company in St. Thomas, U.S. Virgin Islands. Rubin was offered a managerial position in the company, and so he and my mom decided to move to St. Thomas. At that time, I had just finished my freshman year at Bronx Science. I had friends, I was on the swimming team, and, most importantly, for a fifteen-year-old boy, I had a girlfriend, Judy.

So when they decided to move to St. Thomas, I moved in with my dad, who lived pretty much in the same neighborhood, on the upper west side. I took the subway every day from Manhattan to the upper Bronx. Even though I stayed in the city, I did have some great vacations visiting Mom and Rubin in St. Thomas. I even spent a summer there, working in the plant he was managing.

Shortly after my mom and stepfather moved, they became friends with the head manager of the company and his wife, who were Bahais. The Bahais followed the teachings of a man named Baha'u'llah, who lived in the 1800s in Persia (present day Iran), and they believed that he was the prophet for "this age." They believe that all the "prophets" from other religions that ever lived were manifestations of God in their respective ages. To them,

Moses, Jesus, Mohammed and Buddha, are all equal, and now this man Baha'u'llah is the prophet for this age. Mom and Rubin said that they had a revelation that this was true and made a commitment to join.

To become a Bahai is simple. Once you believe this to be true, you just sign a card, and you are in! The summer I was there, I went with them to a couple of meetings, and I was invited to join. At that stage in my life, I was pretty much an agnostic or atheist, so the idea of joining this other religion was not really the direction I wanted to go.

Back home in New York, the upper west side was not as glamorous as now. It was just another neighborhood of mixed ethnicities in Manhattan. There were Jews, blacks, Puerto Ricans, Italians and Irish, but mostly they all seemed to get along. Living with my dad was definitely different. He had a very active social life; so it was like two bachelors living together. He had the business, the Olympic Swim School, that he took over from Zsigo a few years earlier. And he dated.

Having grown up in Vienna and with all his piano lessons in his youth, Dad returned to taking piano lessons and playing. He had me take lessons with his same piano teacher for a couple of years. However, I was more interested in sports and rock and roll than classical piano. My dad's piano teacher was definitely old school, and there was no room for anything but the classics. After a couple of years, I dropped the piano lessons. I had previously also taken guitar lessons but did not stick to that either. I don't think Dad was too happy about me choosing sports over music.

I did appreciate some of the classics, but I was definitely getting into the rock and roll explosion happening then with the "British invasion"—the Beatles, the Rolling Stones, the Who, and others. I was also starting to get into the folk music scene, with Bob Dylan and Joan Baez. But every time I would get in the car with Dad, it was either opera or classical piano on the radio. All the same, Dad and I got along fine. He was a good cook, and I especially loved when we would go to Uncle Leon's butcher shop, and he would load us up with awesome meats that he cooked. We ate well. I still use some of the recipes I learned from him. After all, growing up in Vienna, he was exposed to all kinds of sophisticated cuisine, music, and arts.

Some things Dad was into rubbed off on me, which I appreciated; others I didn't. What did rub off on me was something I really didn't understand until much later—a level of snobbery that comes as a result of growing up with German/Austrian Jewish parents. Later in life, I recognized that I did carry a sense of arrogance because of our family background. We looked down on others, especially other Jews that were from Poland. We were the sophisticated Jews, not like the poor ones (even though our ancestors too originated from Poland). Another aspect of that culture is a certain stiffness and a lack of affection. We would kiss, but do it more as a formality, and I never heard the words "I love you" from either my mom or dad growing up.

German Jews have a certain reputation. They are known as *Yekkes*. It is not clear what the word actually means, but, generally speaking, the Yekke is known to be very formal, organized, and arrogant compared to Jews from other lands. I never knew any of this growing up, it was just the way we were. Yekkes are fastidious about punctuality and attention to detail, and are easily irritated when these things are not observed. We were the cultured, more educated Jews. After all, we came from the cultural centers of Berlin and Vienna, and we settled in Manhattan, the "real" New York, unlike the lower classes of Jews that settled in Brooklyn. This arrogance would follow me into adulthood, and into my future relationships, especially with Gloria, whose family background and culture were as opposite to mine as one could ever imagine.

As far as religious practice in my life was concerned at this point, it was nonexistent. I really didn't want to have anything to do with Judaism—I pretty much had enough of it in yeshiva, and felt now that I didn't need anything. If you would have asked me where or who God was at this point, I would probably have said, "I don't know," or "I don't care;" "He isn't real," or "I can't be bothered"—or all of the above. Basically, I didn't have room for God in my life.

So, during those high school years, I pretty much came and went as I pleased. Manhattan was easy to get around via the subways and buses. My high school girlfriend, Judy, lived in a place called City Island, which was an island in the Bronx. She came from a somewhat stable Jewish family, and I felt at home with her and her parents. Once again, I was drawn to a "normal" family dynamic, which I did not have, but missed. She was very smart and helped me quite a bit with homework and such. I did all right in school, but I was more of a jock than a nerd. The school was full of brainy kids because of its emphasis on science and math. There was a computer room with these giant machines, and, in retrospect, it would have been a good idea for me to take computer science, which I thought at the time was definitely for nerds only. My interest was more in the area of social studies, history, and politics. It was in my high school years that my liberal/radical leanings became more developed.

SPORTS

Dad taught me how to swim at the age of seven, and I began to swim competitively in AAU (Amateur Athletic Union) swim meets. I loved swimming, but the swim meets were scary for me at that age. I was a good swimmer but it would have been better if I had stuck with it and been consistent.

I also loved other sports. I played football, basketball, and baseball, and would go to Central Park and play with other kids, or at school. I especially liked basketball because I was taller than the rest of the kids in my class. By the time I was in 7th grade, I was around 5'10", while my brother was 6'2". However, I stopped growing shortly after that, only growing about another inch. Through 7th and 8th grade, still at the yeshiva, we had a junior high basketball team that I played on, and we played other schools.

So when I got into Bronx Science, I thought I would naturally play basketball. But before the basketball tryouts, I saw a notice about swimming tryouts. My interest was piqued, so I thought I would see, if maybe I could do both. Even though I had not really been swimming for a couple of years, I ended up setting a record for the fastest tryout time, and the coach immediately put me on the team. I felt very welcome, even though I was the youngest member of the team. Back then, most kids went to junior high schools up to 9th grade, then on to high school. But kids in private schools went straight from 8th grade into high school. So I was a freshman in high school, which had mostly kids from private and religious schools.

I swam for four years in high school. We always had a good team. The way it worked was that there was the regular season where we would have dual meets with the other public high schools in the Bronx; then at the end of the season there was a big meet over a couple of days where all the swimmers in the city would compete in the city championships. There were individual as well as team championships. In my freshman year, we almost won the city championship had it not been for a disqualification of our freestyle relay, because one of the swimmers took off too soon. That was such a disappointment. That was as close as we would come over the four years that I swam for the team that we would win the city championship. We did win our Bronx division one year.

In each city championship meet, I would swim the 200-yard freestyle. That was my best event, and eventually, in my senior year, I won the city championship in that event, posting my best time and setting a school record. I went on that year to the regional championships, and while I didn't win, I did set another school record. I always wanted Dad to watch me swim, but at most meets he was busy working. I remember him watching the finals of my 200 in my senior year and looking up at the stands and seeing him there. That meant a lot to me. We had a good relationship, but often we were into our own lives, he with the business, his music, his social life, and me with school, swimming, my friends, and especially my girlfriend.

At the same time that I was swimming in high school, Dad trained me in the method that he and Zsigo had developed, so I worked in the club as a lifeguard and an instructor. I also had the opportunity to teach private lessons.

When it came time to apply to colleges, I went to the University of Wisconsin, simply because my brother had gone there. It was already known as a bastion of radicalism, which suited me well at that time. I also planned on being on the swim team, which I started out doing. However, little things like pot and drinking interfered with my swimming, so I naturally quit the swim team after just a few weeks of training before the season.

CHAPTER 8
POLITICS, PROTESTS, AND PARTIES

I have been interested in politics my whole life. Starting back in 1956, when I was six years old, I went around in our apartment building hanging door hangers for Adlai Stevenson running for president. All my family were Democrats, as were 99 percent of Jewish people in that day, while the Republican Party was seen as a party of rich, white elites, WASPs (White Anglo-Saxon Protestants).

In 1964, when Barry Goldwater ran against President Johnson, the whole family was all in for Johnson. We thought that Goldwater would get us into a war based on the ads the Democrats were putting out that he was a threat to peace, even though Johnson would later get us deeper and deeper into the Vietnam war with no end in sight. The only person in our family that voted for Goldwater was Uncle Leon, and we all thought he was crazy. I remember a huge family argument about this.

A few years later in 1968, I worked in Eugene McCarthy's campaign. He was a senator from Minnesota who was an early and vocal opponent of the Vietnam war. During my senior year, I became radicalized, and while previously supporting and towing the line of the Democratic war narrative, I started to turn against it, as did many of my generation and even established Democrats. There were protests against the war, including a large one that took place in Central Park, Manhattan, which I participated in. There was a growing movement against the war.

In that year, there were two major assassinations that tore at the fabric of our country. On April 4, 1968, Martin Luther King, Jr., the great civil rights leader and pastor, was killed in Memphis, Tennessee. Two months later, on June 6, Bobby Kennedy was killed. He had decided to run for president earlier that year. Johnson had decided not to run again for president, and that left Hubert Humphrey, a former senator from Minnesota who was Johnson's vice president. The Republicans put up Richard Nixon, who had been vice president under Dwight Eisenhower in the 1950s. His political career was thought to have been over, but he came back to secure the nomination in 1968, promising to end the war. He was elected that November. The country was fed up with the ongoing war in Vietnam. They were against not only its cost but also the loss of so many young men who were drafted and shipped off to war, and were killed in what seemed like a hopeless and endless war.

When I was off to college, I participated in several marches and protests in Madison, Wisconsin, already known to be a liberal bastion. Some of the protests got somewhat violent, like smashing windows, though I never participated in any of the violent aspects of the protests. The National Guard was called out on a couple of occasions. In August 1970, there was a bombing of Sterling Hall of the Army Math Research Center in which one person was killed. That put a stop to the protests. At this point, I had already left Madison to take "a semester off," and had gone out to Colorado. That semester off lasted twenty years until I did go back to college at Colorado Christian University, and finally earned my Bachelor's degree. It was years later that I got involved in politics again, this time as a Republican. My "awakening" happened in 1980, after four years under Jimmy Carter. I voted Republican for the first time, for Ronald Reagan, and I have voted that way ever since.

While I was in college in Madison, I started partying pretty early on. I also worked at an Italian restaurant called Lorenzo's, in the kitchen washing dishes. It was a job my brother had when he went to UW years before (remember, he was my idol and I did everything that he did). I started drinking beer along with a lot of the college kids, and I was also smoking pot. My introduction to pot happened in the summer of 1968, after high school. My brother, who had moved out to San Francisco previously and had embraced the hippie lifestyle, gave me some pot, and along with Judy, and another couple that were friends from school, we all "turned on" together.

My involvement with drugs, and getting high, and dealing went on for the next twelve years. While in college, I tried LSD and Mescaline several times. While I never had a bad "trip," I certainly witnessed others having lasting bad trips.

During college, I had a few romantic flings, but my main interest was getting high, drinking, and hanging out. School was definitely not a priority. After three semesters at the University of Wisconsin, I went out to Colorado with a couple of other people. The drive out there was interesting. I had met a local girl, Karin, and convinced her to join us on this journey out to Colorado. I had bought a used Vauxhall (I know, I had never heard of it either; it's a British car) for $50. We loaded up some of our belongings and headed west for the 1000-mile trek to Boulder, Colorado. Along the way, somewhere in Iowa, the car died. It was at night, and somehow we were able to connect with a guy who owned a used car lot, and he sold me an old Plymouth station wagon for $100. With that, we made it the rest of the way to Boulder. I immediately fell in love with the mountains and the dry, clean air, and most of all, the free flow of marijuana that our friends from college had access to.

It wasn't too long after arriving in Boulder in 1970 that I knew that I wasn't going back to Wisconsin anytime soon. For one thing, I hated the winters there. The cold, the wind, the snow, and the ice never left all season long, and you rarely saw the sun. It was actually quite depressing. Boulder was quite different; even winter days could be mild and sunny. So in a short time, Karin and I connected with a few other people, and we formed a sort of "commune" and shared a house together.

Our common bond was that we smoked pot every day and hung out with others who enjoyed the same lifestyle. For me, smoking pot was a great escape from the pain and hurt of the past that I carried. Of course, I didn't realize that at the time. All I knew then was that it felt good, it was cool, and I had a good time with friends hanging out, getting high, and listening to rock music.

Boulder at the time time was a magent for hippies. The mountains were certainly a draw, and the free flow of pot and other drugs helped as well. It was also a center for the New Age, which I was drawn to as well. This included astrology, Tarot cards, yoga, meditation, and the yin/yang of the microbiotic diet which I also embraced. It filled the spiritual void in my life that I didn't know I had, and worked well with getting high. It was "the Age of Aquarius" in my life that lasted for several years.

The only problem I had was money. That had always been a challenge for me. Growing up, a lot of the arguments in the house were over money. Mom and Dad were very different in their views of money. I tended to take after my dad in that regard. But based on the stationery experience, I did worry about money. I was never really taught about money, except that it's good to have it and basically spend it on whatever you want in the moment. The issue of money and finances would be a source of conflict for me in the years to come as well. However, it didn't take me long to find a solution to enable to maintain my lifestyle.

CHAPTER 9
THE "PHARMACEUTICAL" BUSINESS

So here I am, hanging out in Boulder, letting my hair grow—I had what is called a Jew-fro. I did get a job working at an IHOP, washing dishes. By this time, my hair was pretty long, and the manager wanted me to stay in the kitchen so as not to offend any of the customers. Also, about this time, I realized that there were "business" opportunities in the world of pot—better than dish-washing. And, like most good Jews, why buy retail? So, I would buy a couple of pounds at a time and start selling bags to make enough to pay for my own supply. During this time, I realized that I had a market for my product back in Wisconsin with my college buddies too, all of whom were now regularly smoking pot. I would buy a few pounds at first, then drive back to Madison, sell it to my friends, and then drive back.

Around this time, I discovered a town in the mountains called Estes Park. It was about 45 minutes from Boulder, and it was near the entrance to Rocky Mountain National Park. Since I was now a big-time pot dealer (just kidding; pretty small time, really), I thought it best to not live in the city around all the other pot heads and dealers. It was safer to live in a remote area, and this was perfect. So I rented a small, one room cabin and set up life there. To fill out the mountain life, I got a dog, a beautiful husky mix, and named him Samson.

CHAPTER 9: THE "PHARMACEUTICAL" BUSINESS

There was one year that I took a car trip from Colorado to New York. At that time, I had a Chevy pickup. I was into my cowboy identity, wearing cowboy hat, boots—the works! As a kid growing up in the city, I was always intrigued by cowboys. I watched *The Lone Ranger* and *Roy Rogers* on TV, and played with cap guns that I would wear around the house. Now I was living out my childhood dreams!

So I drove back to New York with Samson in the back of the pickup and made it to the family gathering for the Passover *seder* that was at my Uncle Leon and Aunt Anita's house in Long Island. The seder had just begun when I made my entrance, with Samson. My uncle was not pleased that we, especially Samson, had disrupted the event. He was not a dog lover at that time. He made me put Samson back in the truck, where he stayed the rest of the evening. Years later, though, he changed. At that time, he was driven, restless, and at times grouchy. After some hardships, he definitely mellowed out, and even had dogs himself. Years later, he would apologize to me for reacting the way he did to Samson being in the house. He later had his own dog, a golden retriever that became part of the family.

In the summer of 1971, my dad, who was very disappointed that I had dropped out of college, offered to pay for a trip for me to Europe. My brother was going with his girlfriend at the time, and he thought maybe we could either go together or connect there. So, with a backpack, I flew overseas, arranging to meet up with Ron and his girlfriend, in Morocco of all places. Why Morocco? For me, because it was known to have some of the best hashish. The trip overall was not a great experience. I was sick most of the time, with terrible diarrhea, probably from drinking the water and smoking too much hash. The toilets there consisted of a hole in the floor with a place for each foot on either side. Not a good situation in the condition I was in. Also, we took a boat from Morocco to the island of Ibiza, and I got terribly sea sick. Not a lot of fun. I was eager to get back home after about two weeks.

After returning to the States, I spent that summer in New York working at Dad's club, staying at his apartment while he went to Europe. I had a blast that summer!

After returning to Estes Park, I resumed my career in dealing. I also made some like-minded friends who were living there. One couple, Don and Rhoda, lived right in town. We would hang out together, get high, and drink. One night there happened to be an eclipse of the moon, and in our pot-induced state, we hatched the idea to open a gift shop in Estes Park, named Eclipse Imports. So we went into business together. In the shop, we sold pot paraphernalia, but also imported items like some clothes and little wood carved household items from India and such.

Around this time, I met Judy, who lived next door to them, and we started "dating" and hanging out together. She was coming off another relationship, and we just sort of hit it off. The fact that we both liked to get high helped as well. So after a short time, she moved in with me. Judy had a dog named "She-dog," who got along great with Samson. That was our family for the first couple of years.

One day I walked into our store only to find that there was a smashed display case and broken glass on the floor. My first thought was, "Oh no, we've been broken into!" But I quickly realized that this was not the case because the lock was not broken. After calling Don, I found out that he and Rhoda had a drunken fight in the store the night before and that he had somehow managed to smash the display cabinet. Although I had been around drunk people, and I had on several occasions had too much to drink, this was my first encounter with any kind of drunken violent behavior. We had a serious chat, and I bought out their share of the business. From then on, Judy and I ran the business together. Then we decided to get married.

In the Bahai faith, all adherents are considered clergy or priests. So guess who married us? Yes, my mother. On December 31, 1972, so I could get the tax deduction for the year—not that I had legit-imate income I was reporting but it seemed to make sense. My mom performed a simple marriage ceremony in our own cabin. My brother was best man and "maid of honor." After the ceremony, we enjoyed some good pot and beer to celebrate.

At the same time, I continued to deal drugs, but now on a higher scale. (No pun intended.) My connection was with a couple of guys, Greg and Tommy, who were getting their pot directly from Mexico. They lived about an hour away from Estes Park. I had bought an older Ford Galaxie with a great big trunk for the purpose of hauling bricks of pot. I would pick up thirty or forty "bricks," each weighing around a kilo (2.2 pounds), from them and drive to Wisconsin and distribute the pot there.

Over the course of my "pharmaceutical" career, I did have a few close brushes with the law and one serious one. Before I had the big Ford Galaxie, I had an old VW Beetle. One time when I was driving pot back to Wisconsin in it, I had about ten bricks in a duffle bag in the space behind the back seat, and put a bag of dog food on top of it and had Samson in the back seat. He was still a pup. We took off from Boulder and, on the way to the Interstate, went through a small town, where we were pulled over by the local police. It's not that I didn't draw attention to myself, with the long hair and driving the old VW. The cop had me pull into a service station to do a safety test, which back then apparently was the thing. Samson stayed in the back seat. I have to get out so they can put the car up on the lift. I am holding my breath, wondering if they will see or smell the pot in the back, and I am going to end up in jail. Thankfully, the car passed inspection, and I was able to get back on the road with the payload intact, avoiding a search of the car, and make it to Wisconsin and take care of business.

Another near disaster also happened closer to home. I had a friend who had come from Wisconsin to pick up a load of bricks. We went and got them, and they were in the trunk of the car. We stopped in the small town of Nederland near where my contacts were. We were going to go into a local bar for a beer and decided to light up while in the car. We were sitting in the car outside smoking a joint when there was a knock on the window. Low and behold, as I looked out, a local police officer was standing there! We put the joint out and opened the window. There was obviously smoke coming out when I opened the window, but he did not seem to be bothered by it. He could easily have had us get out of the car, search it, and find the motherload in the trunk. Thankfully, he just told us we couldn't park there, and we moved on.

The next brush with the law did not end well. It was August 1973. Judy and I were still running the shop. I was still in the other business, where the "real" money was. My brother at the time also dabbled in the business, and he had a friend who had smuggled a large quantity of hashish from Morocco, of only fair quality. So, I helped move the product. I had a friend, Kelly, who had a friend of a friend—you get the picture. I drove our pick-up truck with Kelly down to Boulder to meet the friend of the friend who was going to purchase ten pounds of the product. It turned out that the friend of the friend of the friend was a federal narcotics agent. Kelly and I were hanging around outside the house while the deal was going down inside so as not to directly meet the "customer." In a few minutes, we were surrounded by DEA agents with guns pointed at us. We were taken to Denver, where we spent the night and were bailed out the next day. The charge was distribution of marijuana. Apparently, there were no specific federal laws about hashish, which is a concentrated form of marijuana.

So now the legal process began. We each had to get lawyers. My lawyer was a young guy, and our legal strategy was this: since I did not personally know the friend of my friend, or the friend of the friend who turned out to be an informer that was working with the federal agents, I was just giving my friend a ride on a sunny summer day. The trial in federal court in Denver was about six months later. During the intervening time, my lawyer suggested that I get a legitimate job so that, in case I got convicted, I could show that I was rehabilitating myself, and maybe stay out of prison.

So, I decided to go to real estate school and get my real estate license. The day of the trial came. We had a jury that was picked, and the main witness was the snitch, the friend of the friend of the friend, who had previously met Kelly, but not me. So My defense that I was just giving my friend a ride seemed to convince the jury. But the case against Kelly was pretty cut and dried. He got convicted, and I was acquitted. What a relief! Had I been convicted, I would most likely have gone to prison. The judge gave Kelly five years of probation because he came from a stable family background and he had served in the military. Since I had neither, had I been convicted, I would have almost certainly served time in federal prison. Even having an arrest record at times has caused some issues for me.

You would think that with all that I would have ended my drug dealing career. At this point, I was still married to Judy, and we still owned the Eclipse Imports gift shop. We had recently bought a small summer cabin near Allenspark from the profits of our business (not the import shop business, the other one). Allenspark is a small mountain town about fifteen miles from Estes Park, in an area called Meeker Park, at the base of Mt. Meeker and a half mile on a dirt road off of the main road. The cabin was at 8,500 feet above sea level, and it only had summer water and no central heating, just a fireplace and we installed a wood burning heater. There were no year-round residents in the area, and in the winter, the snow piled up. It was situated on a stream, and of course it was perfect in the summer; winter was another issue. When it started getting cold, we had to turn off the summer water, and then we would haul water in containers from the creek for drinking, cooking, and washing. We used the wood stove for heat, and for showers, we would go into Allenspark, where there were public showers. Basically, we were hippies, trying to live in the wild.

As I mentioned earlier, growing up in New York City I always loved watching westerns. I had cap guns and fancied myself a cowboy. When we bought the cabin, my dream was to have horses to complete the picture and we eventually had two horses. We also bought a new 1973 Ford 34 ton 4-wheel drive pickup, a big step up from the old Chevy pickup. We also had a snowplow to keep our road clear since we were a half mile back from the main road. One horse eventually died, and we gave the other one away.

After living together for about a year and then being married for about a year, we thought that Judy could not get pregnant. Then, lo and behold, she does, and Sammi was born on June 6, 1974. At this time, we were deep into using and selling drugs, and at the same time, were very much into living the "back to the land" lifestyle, such as eating healthy, cutting our own wood, and riding our horses. When it came to childbirth, we were going to do it the "natural way." At that time, there was no hospital in Estes Park, but we consulted a country doctor, Sam Luce and decided to have the baby at home. So as Judy went into labor, I thought the logical thing would be to have a party. I called up a few of our fellow hippie types living around us to come over and party, while the baby came. So a few of us hung out in the living room of our cabin drinking and getting high, while Judy was in the bedroom with our midwife going through labor. After laboring pretty much all day, her water would not break.

We called Dr. Luce, and he came up and, after examining her, said that he needed to break her water but could not do it at our place because of the lack of a sterile environment. We had to take her into town to his clinic to finish the birth process. Would you believe it at around 5:00 p.m. on that day, it was snowing! Wait, in June? Yes, we were living at 8,500 feet, so it could snow anytime of the year, although it was unusual in the summer.

So we loaded her into the back of a friend's station wagon and took her the fifteen miles into town to the clinic. There, Dr. Luce delivered our firstborn, a girl. We named her Sammi after Dr. Luce. We were ecstatic to have a baby. Many of our friends in the area were having babies around the same time.

Around that time, we met a couple, John and Laura Bernstein (not their real names). John was a friend of Ron's girlfriend's brother at the time, and he was also a drug dealer. The four of us hit it off, and we would hang out together and get high. He had the best cocaine, which we were now using pretty regularly. They were living in Estes Park, and we would hang out together, get high, go out to dinner, and generally have a good time.

One day, they came to us with a proposal. They had a connection in Colombia, South America, for pure cocaine, and came up with a plan to smuggle it into the country. Laura's dad owned a factory that made aerosol cans for hair spray and other uses. John came up with a way to fill these cans with cocaine and just have a little vial in the can that would spray whatever product was supposed to be in the can but it was mostly filled with cocaine. The plan was that we would go on a cruise out of Miami, and one of the stops would be in Cartegena, Colombia. There, we would be picked up while the ship was docked in port, and everyone went off to go sightseeing. A taxi driver would take us to meet up with John, where we would be given the cans of cocaine and be taken back to the ship. The idea was that since customs coming back from cruises was very minimal, it should be no problem getting the "product" back into the country, then flying it in our luggage back to Colorado.

When presented with this scheme, we thought, "Hey, why not? A free cruise and the opportunity to make some extra cash!" So, we did, and it went off without a hitch. In fact, it went so well, we did it a second time. This time, though, in order to bring a larger quantity, the plan was to get suitcases that had fabric linings that could be pulled back, and bags of cocaine could be put under the linings and sewed back in. More product, more profit, so why not?

At this point, Sammi was about six months old. We took her to my mom's, who had divorced Rubin and was living alone in Texas. She knew what we were up to but was not particularly upset that we were smuggling cocaine. She had actually joined us in smoking pot on several occasions, so it was not too big of a deal for her. Looking back, how crazy was this! Had we gotten caught smuggling cocaine, we could have lost everything. I had already been arrested for distribution. I was working a "legitimate" job as a real estate agent, and we could have lost custody of Sammi and much more.

On the second trip, there were a couple of touch-and-go moments while we were in Cartagena. We went with the tour bus, and at one of the stops at a hotel gift shop, we were handed a wicker bag. It contained some blankets, and wrapped in the blankets were the bags of cocaine that we were supposed to carry back on the ship, insert the bags into the lining of our suitcases, and close them up. So after the "hand off," we got back on the tourist bus, and were driving back to the ship, and there just so happened to be some kind of street protest or military operation going on. There were tanks in the street with soldiers patrolling. We overheard a couple of the other tourists on the bus talking, and one said, "They're probably looking for drug dealers," which immediately sent waves of panic through me. Fortunately, we made it back without issue, and the trip was a success. Eventually, my mom got interested and ended up going on a couple of these trips herself!

After the precariousness of these trips, I pretty much wound down my business in dealing, although I continued to use the stuff pretty regularly. That included pot, hash, and cocaine. And drinking was always in that mix as well.

CHAPTER 9: THE "PHARMACEUTICAL" BUSINESS

Less than a year later, Judy became pregnant again, and Seth, our second child, was born on February 13, 1976. By this time, the new Estes Park hospital was built, and he was one of the first babies to be born there. This time we nearly didn't make it to the hospital because the labor went so fast.

CHAPTER 10
BAD IDEAS GONE GOOD

About this time, we decided we needed to expand the cabin, as it would definitely not be big enough to raise two children. The expansion project included adding a second story with two bedrooms and a bath; extending the downstairs; a new roof, a new exterior, and more. Basically, we were building a new house around the existing cabin. While the construction was underway, we had to move out of the house for a time, and we rented a small house in Estes Park. Then things between Judy and me began to go wrong.

She had taken a job as a bartender at a local hot spot in Estes, the Miner's Kettle. We were still getting high and drinking. I had gotten my real estate broker's license and had opened my own office. While Judy was working at the Miner's Kettle, typically she would watch the kids during the day, and I would take care of them after work while she worked at the bar. Oftentimes, they might fall asleep in the car, and we would both be in the bar drinking, having after hours parties, and snorting cocaine.

After the house was livable though not finished, we moved back in. We still had no heat but continued to use a wood burning stove to heat the house. One day on Judy's day off, we took the kids to lunch at the Miner's Kettle. We were friends with the owner as well as everyone that worked there. However, we weren't familiar with the waitress who came over to us to take our order. She was this cute little young lady and spoke with the thickest southern accent I'd ever heard. I could barely understand her. As she walked away after taking our order, I turned to Judy and wondered aloud where Dave (the owner) had gotten "this one." We had a good laugh about her accent and manner. Such a hick! Her name was Gloria. Yes, that's Gloria. This was in the fall of 1977.

As time went on, Gloria and Judy became friends, and we all partied together. On New Year's Eve, there was this big party at the Kettle, and at midnight, everyone was going around kissing each other and doing the New Year's thing. Most of us were totally sloshed. When Gloria and I kissed, something happened that we later would refer to as "The kiss that was heard around the world!"

Over the next few months, Judy would work nights. She would bring the kids into town to the Kettle, and I would come over after work, have a beer or two, then take the kids home to Allenspark. As time went on, Judy would stay out later and later; I knew she was partying and doing drugs. Eventually, I suspected that she was doing more than that. One night she didn't come home until the morning, and I knew that she had been with someone; in fact, she admitted it. I should not have been surprised, as she had, over the time we were married, hinted at the idea of "open marriage," of which I was not a fan.

In any case, this was extremely hurtful. We had a big fight over it; we had been fighting quite a bit anyway. I realized later that my passivity was a contributing factor to the breakdown, and there were dynamics that flowed from my own parents' divorce that factored in. I was later to understand that promiscuity, adultery, and the breakdown of families was a generational pattern, even going back a couple of generations that I knew of.

But at this point, I was hurt, confused, and angry. My way of dealing with anger typically was to "stuff it" and go passive. I had learned that early in life. Later that day, while I was in town,

I ran into Gloria. We had become friends by this time, but nothing physical had happened—except for "the kiss."

Gloria wound up in Colorado by happenstance. She was living in Memphis, TN, and dating a guy, and they decided to go to Masoula, Montana, on vacation. So they hit the road, and when they got to Colorado, they remembered that there were a couple of kids from their hometown in Greenwood who had gone out to Estes Park, so they decided to stop in and see them. They hung out for a while, and then Bubba (yeah, that's his real name) her boyfriend, decided that they were out of money and needed to return to Memphis. At that point, Gloria, being the adventurous soul that she is, said, "No, I am going to stay here." So she did. The next day she got the job and the Miner's Kettle, and the rest ... well you know.

So I shared with Gloria about Judy staying out all night, probably with someone else. Her street-wise advice was, "Well, you could do the same thing." So that night Judy was off and stayed home with the kids and I spent the evening hanging out with Gloria and spent the night with her. When I came back the next morning, Judy packed a bag and left, leaving the kids. At this time, Sammi was four and Seth was two. Seth took it the hardest; Sammi was more easy-going and went with the flow.

The kids stayed with me for the next couple of months, while Judy, who was living in town, would pick them up on weekends. Most of the time, when she would come to get them, Gloria was with me. Judy was not happy about this and was jealous. She told me once she wanted to get back together. I was not interested. Eventually, in the divorce settlement, I agreed to give her primary custody, and the kids would have weekends and holidays with me. I later regretted giving up custody of the kids. I was selfishly enjoying my time and justified my position by thinking *Kids are better off with mothers.*

From then on, Gloria and I hung out together either at her place in town, or at my place in the mountains. She was a lot of fun, different than any other girl I had been with. It wasn't just the fact that she was from such a different background and upbringing than me, but that she was sweet, caring and exciting to be around. But one thing I noticed is that, when she had too much to drink—which could be just a couple of drinks—she could become belligerent or incoherent. The morning after, she typically would not remember what happened. I later learned that this was called being a "blackout drinker," conscious but not aware of what was happening or what was being said.

One night we were leaving from an after-hours party at the Kettle; it was around 3:00 a.m. I usually do not get drunk, but this night I felt that I was unable to drive, so Gloria drove. The drive to the house was about fifteen miles through winding roads. Just outside of town, there was a particularly sharp corner, and we were going too fast. She missed the turn, and the car went off the road, down an embankment, flipping end over end, and landing upside down on the roof. After we landed, I looked over to the driver's seat, and Gloria was not there. She had been thrown through the windshield out into a field at the bottom of the hill. With pulsating adrenaline, I was able to pull myself out of the car, and while I was banged up, I seemed to be okay. I found Gloria laying in the field, obviously hurt badly. The reality sank in that we had drugs in the car, both pot and cocaine, and that the sheriff would be coming at some point. The cocaine was easily disposed of, but I couldn't find the bag of pot that I knew was in the car as it was sitting upside down on its roof. We needed help. I remembered there was a camp ground back up on the road that I knew had a phone booth. I managed to walk up the hill that we had just rolled down and walk to the phone booth. I did not have any change, so I was hoping to find a dime somewhere. I got to the phone booth, and there was a quarter in the coin return.

The first person I thought to call was Margo. She worked for me in the real estate office, and she and her husband were also friends. I told her what had happened and asked her if she could help. She and Bob came right away. They arrived around the same time as the sheriff. I told Margo right away that there was a bag of marijuana somewhere that we needed to find before the sheriff came and before they towed the car. Our story was that there was a deer in the road, and we had swerved to avoid it and went off the road. When the sheriff came, Margo asked him for a flashlight, and she hurriedly came down with it. When she shone the light into the car, we immediately saw the bag of pot, sitting right there on the upside down ceiling. I immediately grabbed the bag and scattered its contents out in the field.

An ambulance finally came, and I rode with Gloria to the hospital. It turned out she had a torn ACL in her knee and a collapsed lung. I was just a little bruised up. There was never a breath test, or any question of whether we were drinking or using drugs. At this point in my real estate career, I was established in the town with a good reputation, even though some knew of my prior drug arrest, which I always portrayed as being an innocent bystander. I was thankful not to tarnish my reputation.

I was still an atheist, but I did consider us to be extremely lucky in that this accident: we could have easily been killed or seriously injured. We could have been arrested. None of that happened. But, looking back on this and all the other experiences of doing drugs, having brushes with the law, and generally doing crazy things, it was obvious that the hand of God was over me protecting me through it all. He knew me and loved me even when I was far, far away from Him. He always had a plan for me, but I wouldn't know it until sometime later, I just thought that someone or something was definitely looking out for me.

As with all my brushes with disaster, I didn't really learn the lesson. As a result of the accident and other issues in our relationship, Gloria and I decided to take a little break. Gloria was different than any girl I had ever known, and she had become so special to me. She grew up in a small town in Mississippi, the oldest of four, with two sisters and a brother. Raised as a Southern Baptist, she went to church every Sunday and Sunday night as well as Wednesday nights. As she puts it, it was a lot of religion without relationships. She was brought up with the core belief that "God is watching you, and He will punish you if you step out of line."

I also did not know the hurt and abuse that Gloria had endured at a very young age. It was only later that I learned any of the details. Up to now, all I knew was that she was fun; she was different than Judy, and she cared very much about me and I liked to hang out with her. At the same time, she was also not well educated and was quite naïve about a lot of things. She had graduated high school but had not gone to college. But, she was outgoing and fun and liked to party, and that was enough for me. Little did I know but there was something deeper that kept drawing us back together.

The accident took place in the fall of 1978. Not long after, Gloria decided to go back to Memphis, where she had lived prior to coming to Colorado. We were still getting together off and on, but she had friends in Memphis and was talking about going back to school.

Gloria was so different from me. We joke sometimes about our story: "Mississippi redneck meets stiff-necked New York Jew in Colorado." People often ask, "Where did you meet? You seem like such a cool couple."

Our response: "Oh, we met in a bar. I was married. She was the 'other woman' and it was sex, drugs, and rock and roll—we don't recommend it."

Gloria was raised in a fairly poor working-class family where there was a lot of drama, especially with her mom. Her mom grew up in poverty and, at age eighteen enlisted in the Air Force during the Korean War. Coming back home afterward, she met Fred, who worked for the electric company. They got married, and about six months later, Gloria was born. Besides the math not adding up, there is more to the story and how it impacted Gloria's identity. Gloria's mom, Bonnie, developed health issues early on. She was a drinker and brought a lot of emotional drama to the family when the kids were young. After a few drinks, she would even threaten to leave the family.

I also found out later that Bonnie's father, Gloria's grandfather, was a pedophile and had been sexually abusing Gloria along with an uncle from the age of five to nine years old. That abuse would affect her for many years to come, even causing issues for us in our relationship. Gloria's background of abuse, and oppressive religious indoctrination was a total setup to fall into the pattern of drug and alcohol abuse and sexual promiscuity. Little did I know that her actions were more about simply trying to cover up the pain and shame of her past.

Somehow, in God's sovereign plan, He put us together. Me with my baggage of being raised German Jew—*Yeche* as we are not so affectionately called, with the accompanying pride, arrogance, and general "know it all" attitude, yet the pain of a broken home. Gloria, with her troubled background of sexual abuse and harsh religious upbringing, yet hardworking and industrious. What a combination! It's as if God was taking some raw material, like coal, and with time, pressure, and difficulty, yet with His grace, kindness, and love, producing something beautiful—a couple of diamonds perhaps—but of course still flawed.

So Gloria decides to go back to Memphis, which is pretty close to her hometown of Greenwood, Mississippi. She always brags that she was in Memphis when Elvis died and got to go through the line to see him in the coffin twice. Before coming to Colorado, she had lived there with some friends, which is where she started living the party life after being pretty straight laced through high school. When she left Colorado, we pretty much thought our relationship was over, but we were both open.

One day, not too long after she got to Memphis, I got the call. Gloria was pregnant. I thought that was impossible! She had told me she could not get pregnant, so we never used protection. *How could this happen?* I already had two kids, a successful real estate business, the divorce with Judy settled, and life was good! There was no way I could father a child out of wedlock, and out of state, at this point. Marrying Gloria was not on the radar at all. She was someone I had a fling with; it was fun; we had good chemistry, but being parents together was a non-starter. So I did the only thing I knew, and we made the worst decision of our lives. I told her she had to get an abortion. She didn't argue, and shortly after, went somewhere in Memphis and had it done. We would live to deeply regret that decision.

After a few months in Memphis, Gloria decided to come back to Estes Park. We were keeping in touch over the phone. It was a mutual decision, and we decided to live together. As a result of the divorce, we put the house in Allenspark on the market, although it was never completely finished. Gloria and I rented a house in Estes Park from some friends of ours and set up house together. But things were not so rosy. We picked up where we left off, drinking and drugging. I was still running my real estate company by day, and partying and getting high by night.

Then a friend of mine in the real estate business invited us to a gathering in Denver for a presentation by a group called "Actualizations." The guy who started it had been with a program called E.S.T., a popular self-improvement program at that time, and he had gone off and started something similar. It was all about self-improvement, to "actualize" yourself to be the best you and so on. Gloria and I both got involved and went to several seminars.

Up to this point, there was absolutely no religious involvement by either one of us. Our "church" was the Wheel Bar in downtown Estes Park. Our fellowship was with other drinkers and "druggers." One Sunday, which happened to be Easter, we invited some of the people we'd become friends with through Actualizations up to our house in Estes Park for a little party. We had alcohol, of course, and we were all drinking, or so we thought, and Gloria's behavior, as usual, got a little out of control after a couple of drinks.

The next day she got a call from one of the friends in the group, Jim, who said he wanted to meet her because he had a business opportunity to present. Gloria had just started a job at the local radio station selling advertising. So, she went down to Boulder and met with him. He told her a little about Amway, but, as it turned out, the meeting wasn't about the business opportunity; he was actually doing an intervention with her. He wasn't drinking at the party and noticed her behavior and the signs of alcoholism. He had experienced the same with his own wife, who had gone through treatment and was in AA.

After their meeting, they both came up to Estes Park and walked into my office. He explained to me what he was proposing: that we send Gloria to a treatment center that he knew of in Jordan, Minnesota, outside of the Twin Cities. She would be there for a month, but if after a few days it was determined that she didn't need to be there, she could leave. Of course, that was just part of the sales pitch because he knew very well that she needed to be there for the whole thirty days.

Gloria wanted my approval—what did I think of this? I had no experience or knowledge of the AA program. My idea of an alcoholic was the bums on the streets in the Bowery, lower Manhattan, who drank out of a bottle in a paper bag, or people who had to have a drink in the morning to get by. Gloria was not in that category. However, I knew that Gloria's behavior would change after a couple of drinks, but I didn't make the connection that these were symptoms of alcoholism. It seemed like this was a good idea, but the condition of her going was that I had to come for family week, even though we were not married at the time. I agreed, not really knowing what I was going in for.

The only catch now was that it was going to cost $2,500 plus the airfare. Gloria had been working at the radio station for only a month, but as it turns out her health insurance had just kicked in and they would pay for 80 percent of the cost. Jim was in a group connected to Actualizations called Course of Miracles, and he told them about this girl who needed help to go through treatment, and they collected over $500 to pay the difference and for her airfare. So on May 8, 1981, Jim accompanied Gloria to Jordan, Minnesota, to go through drug and alcohol treatment. And thus began a new life for both of us.

CHAPTER 11
BELIEVING IN A TREE

As part of the family week, I went to the treatment center as Gloria's "significant other." I was so clueless as to what this was about that on the plane ride to Minneapolis, I thought it would be cool to have a couple of drinks. Nobody would know. After we landed, I was met at the airport by Gloria, accompanied by one of the counselors who arranged the transportation. It must have been obvious that I had imbibed. Nothing was said, but I felt the vibe from the counselor. Later, Gloria did mention how inappropriate that was.

My education about the world of AA and addictions was just beginning. Over the next several days at the center, I sat in group settings with other "significant others" who were there for family week as well. We learned about addiction, and about those who enable and also suffer because of the addict's behavior. We watched visual presentations about the physical effects of alcohol and drugs on the liver and other organs. We learned about the diseases related to long-term use of alcohol, and the effects that alcoholism has on the family. We were also introduced to the whole Alcoholics Anonymous program, including Alanon, which is the recovery program for spouses and family members of addicts.

As I started reflecting on Gloria's behavior, it all started to make sense. While she was still young, the effects and behaviors were still present. At this point she was about two weeks into the program, and she was doing great.

The first step in AA is recognizing that you are an addict and that you are powerless over it. Gloria was very cooperative with the program. One of the steps also acknowledges a "higher power," which for most people means God. To me, it meant nothing since I was a professed atheist. *But if Gloria needed a higher power in order to maintain her sobriety, that was fine. But how would that impact me? Was I going to have to buy the God thing too?* I was starting to get nervous about this because they kept pushing the idea that if you are a spouse, or in my case, a "significant other," it would be really important to also follow the twelve steps for Alanon, which is parallel to the AA program.

One of the questions that I began to wonder about was whether I needed to go through treatment myself. In retrospect, I had been high nearly every day since high school graduation. My drug history included LSD, mescaline, peyote, speed, cocaine, and, of course, lots of marijuana and hashish. Add alcohol to all of that and it was a logical question: *Maybe I should be going through the treatment as well.*

One day during "family week," I had a meeting with one of the counselors, as all of the family members were to do. Little did I know that meeting would prove to be life changing for me. I had already been internally processing a lot of the information I was receiving during the various sessions. When I sat down with the counselor, I started the conversation by saying, "I am wondering if I am an addict in need of treatment."

She was gracious and replied, "Why don't you make a commitment to refrain from alcohol and drugs for ninety days and see if it is a problem for you? And, in any case, it will be very difficult for Gloria to stay in the relationship if you continue to use alcohol, and she is trying to stay straight and sober."

I thought for a moment. "Okay, I can see that, so yes, I will make that commitment. However, I have a real problem with this higher power stuff. I am an atheist, you see, so it is very difficult for me to accept this notion of a higher power."

"That's fine, but can you believe in something outside of your-self?" As she spoke, she looked out the window. "Even if it's a tree?"

I was a little confused, but I said, "Okay, I guess I can believe in a tree."

With that "confession of faith," I began my spiritual journey.

My lack of belief in God or any "higher power" was a leftover of my overall rebellious 60s hippie mindset that I still walked in. Not only was I an atheist, but I still had a lot of liberal views on many issues. But I realized that if Gloria was going to succeed in her new life of sobriety—not just "not drinking," but a real change, including this spiritual thing—then I would have to somehow sup-port her. It meant I had major choices to make in two areas of my life: my own drug and alcohol use and this "higher power" issue.

In retrospect, whether she realized it or not, the counselor appealed to me through logic. I have since come to understand that atheism is totally illogical, because the very premise that some-thing can "evolve" out of nothing is already faulty, and the whole idea of atheism, or that we just got here by accident, haphazardly, is totally illogical. So in appealing to my natural sense of logic, she in effect was questioning what I now use to show the illogicality of atheism—the belief that there is no God. That question is: in all the knowledge of the universe, which no human can know, could there be the possibility of a "higher power" or Creator? And, of course, the answer is yes; that knowledge could exist. Therefore, the person is not really an atheist, but an agnostic, meaning, they are not sure of the existence of God. But it is possible.

So there I was, being confronted with a very logical question, "Is there something outside yourself that you can believe in, even if it is a tree?"

My answer at that point was, "Yes, okay, I can believe in something outside myself, and yes, that something I can call a 'higher power.'"

And with that, began the real first step in my spiritual journey. I could now "buy into" the AA/Alanon way of life. That would include going to meetings for myself, and also supporting Gloria in her journey to live a sober life. I cared enough for her to do it.

Thus began a life change, when I returned to Colorado. No more bars, no more getting high, no more alcohol of any kind! We both started going to meetings. We realized that there was a whole world out there of people who didn't drink or do drugs. Imagine that! Up until then, most of our friends were living the same lifestyle as we were, so we thought it was "normal."

I decided to join a running club, and we used to run in races regularly. I started with 5ks, then 10ks, then half marathons, and eventually ran a couple of marathons as well. I was still in the real estate business and was fairly successful so, unbeknownst to Gloria, I bought a beautiful big house that I had previously sold to a couple who decided to resell and move. The couple was older, and they liked me a lot, so I was able to negotiate a very good deal with them. The day came that I blindfolded Gloria and drove her up to the house, and voilà! This was our new home. She was totally blown away, having never lived in a house that nice in her life. Of course, I had not either. It was an amazing house, right in town, with a big yard. It had yellow siding, so it was quickly dubbed "the yellow house." A happy new beginning for us!

I was optimistic about the future, believing that I was going to strike it rich through real estate. Gloria and I were both very involved in AA and Alanon, living in the big yellow house, and enjoying the kids on weekends and vacations. In the divorce settlement, Judy and I had joint custody, but I allowed her to have them during the week, and we would have them every other weekend and on holidays. I lived to regret not fighting to keep them to live with us. It was partly selfish on my part wanting to enjoy my new life. The other reason was that at the time, the prevailing notion was that the kids were better off with their mother. Judy had remarried the same year—as Gloria and I had—to a man named Ron.

I was running pretty much every day, and Gloria was working at a doctor's office. We enjoyed our life and family without drugs or alcohol for the first time, doing things with the kids like hiking in the mountains, roller skating, skiing, and playing games. Life was good and stable.

I was stepping out in my real estate career and got involved in a couple of commercial development deals. One was a campground, and the other was a commercial property. In the campground deal, I was just one of the partners; in the commercial property I spearheaded the deal, gathered a couple of partners, negotiated the sale, and carried the vision for the project. The property was to have office condominiums.

This was around the end of 1979. Jimmy Carter was president, and we had record high inflation and interest rates that went through the roof. Financing opportunities shut down, and we lost everything on both projects. As a result, we were sued by the previous owner of the campground when we could not continue to pay him. We also lost the commercial property deal, and I was sued by one of the partners in that as well. As a result of these losses, I owed money everywhere: to the partners in the commercial property, the bank, and the house, which I could not pay either.

Backing up a couple of years, after my mom divorced Rubin, she was living in Texas where she worked for our friends in the "import business;" then she moved to Estes Park and rented a mobile home. This was around the time that Judy and I were splitting up. However, she did not do well with winters because of her arthritis. So she decided to move to Las Vegas, and she got a job in a casino. In 1982, she was going to be 60. We invited her to come back to Estes to celebrate her birthday with us; my brother Ron was also planning to come. So Gloria had this great idea, "Hey, why don't we get married while your mom and brother are here?"

Yeah, why not? I thought. So I walked into the bank, where I still had good credit, and borrowed some more money, because I knew that I would be rolling in cash as soon as all these great deals started paying off.

CHAPTER 12
TAKE TWO

Gloria and I decided to get married on August 1. It was a Sunday and happened to be Colorado Day. It was held at a very historic location, a famous hotel in Estes Park, called the Stanley Hotel. It was built in the early 1900s by F.O. Stanley, the inventor of the Stanley Steamer autocar. He and his twin brother invented the car and, as the story goes, because of health issues, F.O. founded Estes Park before it was incorporated in the early 1900s. He amazed the local people when he drove up the hill where the hotel was eventually built. Previously, it could only be accessed on horseback.

He then purchased that land and built the hotel, which became a luxury destination for many years. Eventually, the hotel went into receivership, fell into disrepair, and was closed for many years. Then a man named Frank Normali purchased the hotel in 1974 and spent millions repairing it and opening it for business. The Steven King novel, *The Shining*, was inspired by a stay at this historic hotel. In fact, the movie was supposed to be filmed there, but there was no snow on the ground the year they were filming, so they chose another location.

Again, in the early 80s, the property went into bankruptcy, but Frank still owned it and worked on getting it back on its feet. I knew Frank from the Rotary Club and other business gatherings, since I was very active in the community. I was President of the Board of Realtors and President of the Chamber of Commerce as well. So, even though the hotel was closed at the time, I approached Frank about the possibility of having our wedding there. He was agreeable, and, as it turned out, we were the first event at the hotel after it reopened.

Our wedding went off as planned, complete with Sammi as the flower girl and Seth as the ring bearer. Being an upstanding member of the community, I had a lot of friends who came to the wedding. We were also were friends with a Unitarian minister and his wife. At this point, I was still not very God-inclined; it was just "as I understood Him," like the tree. But, in any case, I was not about to have a traditional wedding where God was mentioned. My Jewishness was not really important to me, although even as an atheistic or agnostic Jew, I still celebrated Passover and Chanukah, and, of course, Jesus was not on my radar at all.

So we asked our Unitarian minister friend if he would perform the wedding. There was one condition: no mention of God at the ceremony. Being the good Unitarian that he was, he agreed. I think their theology is something along the lines that there are many ways to get to heaven. That suited me fine. Nevertheless, it was a lot of fun. My whole family came: mom, now twice divorced; Dad with his wife, Maya; my brother Ron; Uncle Walter and Aunt Hannah; Uncle Leon, and Aunt Anita. The contrasts couldn't be more stark. My family was, of course, from Europe and well-traveled. Gloria's parents came from Greenwood, MS, and flying for the first time.

Needless to say, we had some interesting relational dynamics at the wedding. My mom and dad had not seen each other in about twenty years. They both spoke English with German accents. Maya, Dad's wife, was originally from Austria as well. Combine all that with Gloria's parents from Mississippi with their own special accents and you get the picture. We had to translate at times, but everyone was accommodating and did their best to get along. While Mom and Dad didn't really speak much to each other, Mom surprisingly got along better with Maya than anyone else. It certainly was a memorable occasion and so good to have the family together.

We didn't really have a honeymoon. We drove to the next town and stayed at an Inn for the night, then came back the next day. With all the family in town, we felt like we should spend time with them.

Although it was a wonderful visit, the reality of how very different our two worlds were really hit home. Our families and backgrounds couldn't possibly be more opposite. Here we were, not realizing it at the time, two broken people from two vastly different backgrounds and cultures, with vastly different personalities, and experiences, somehow brought together through very unusual circumstances. Of course, we were thinking, like most couples in that moment after the ceremony, that we were going to live "happily ever after."

Boy, were we in for a rude awakening!

IN THE BEGINNING

Gloria decided that "improving her conscious contact with her higher power" meant that she would start going back to church. We've already talked about the sexual abuse she endured as a child as well as her strict religious upbringing. As a result of this horrific abuse, and religious indoctrination depicting a harsh and punishing God, she never felt accepted or loved by Him. Her experience led her to believe that she was a "bad" girl, and that she was "dirty." This was a perfect set up for the life of drugs, alcohol, and promiscuity that she got into after high school and leaving home.

Now sober for a year, married to me, and a part-time stepmom, life was pretty good and seemingly stable. She started going to a local Baptist church because that was all she knew. However, because of her past church experience, she wasn't fully in agreement with the idea of "receiving Jesus." In her mind, she had AA, and that was beyond Jesus. But life went on. She would go to church on Sunday mornings, and I would go on my long weekly run.

There was a couple who attended the church, Chris and Bonnie Thomas. Bonnie was the daughter of Cliff Barrows, the song leader for Billy Graham. Chris was the son of Major Ian Thomas, a British evangelist, who had started several Bible schools around the world. These were "heavy hitters." One of those schools happened to be located just outside of Estes Park, up on a hill called Pole Hill. Bonnie led a women's Bible study every week, which Gloria began to attend. At the end of every session, Bonnie would give an invitation to "receive Jesus" as Savior. Every week when she gave the invitation, Gloria would resist, thinking, *I've been there and done that, now I'm in AA, so I don't need Jesus.*

One day Gloria was invited to a Christian women's luncheon, and Bonnie was the speaker. Bonnie gave her usual invitation in Billy Graham style, "Draw a cross on the back of your name tag if you prayed the prayer of salvation." Gloria prayed the prayer that day and put the cross on the back of her name tag. Life was about to change in a dramatic way!

CHAPTER 13
GLORIA'S ANNOUNCEMENT

After that Bible study, Gloria came bounding into the house, all excited about her decision, and made the famous announcement that would change our lives forever: "I'm born again!"

"Don't bother me with that Jesus stuff," I responded, which was really a reflection of the condition of my heart. This "Jesus stuff" evoked even hostility, as I recalled the hatred of Christians toward Jews over history. I came to realize later that Jewish people are way more aware of Christian antisemitism throughout history than Christians are. Often, when Christians talk to Jewish people about Jesus, they have no clue about the bitterness most Jewish people have towards Jesus, especially those of my generation. To most Jewish people, He is the reason that our people have suffered over the years.

At this time, we were still having Sammi and Seth over on the weekends, and Judy had also remarried earlier that year. When Gloria wanted to take the kids to church, I was not in favor of that. For one thing, when Judy and I were married and had kids, we discussed this and had a brilliant idea. She was raised Catholic and had went to a strict Catholic school. So she did not have a good religious experience. I had no interest in religion either, except for Chanukah and sometimes Passover. In our hippie, pot-and-cocaine-clouded minds, we decided that we wouldn't teach the kids anything about religion. When they were old enough, they could decide for themselves. It seemed logical at the time.

So now Gloria comes to me and wants to take the kids to church. I was not too enthused about the idea, and I especially didn't want to experience the wrath of Judy. Did I mention that she was unpredictable and could be quite nasty? But Gloria's logic won out, which was: "How would they know how to decide if they didn't know anything about God?" Gloria was always, and still is, quite persuasive.

So I thought, *Okay, it can't hurt. When they are with me, I should be able to make that decision.* So Gloria started taking the kids to church, while I would go on my weekly long run.

One day the kids asked Gloria, "How come we have to go to church and Dad doesn't?"

Her answer was, "Dad is Jewish, and Jews don't believe in Jesus." Basically, that was all she knew how to answer them. About the second or third time that they asked her, she replied, "Why don't you ask him yourselves?"

So they did. "Dad, how come we have to go to church and you don't?"

My answer? Well, I didn't have one. In my head, I was going through every reason to tell a nine and seven year-old for not wanting to go to church, and realized that none of my reasons would make any sense to them. So the words that came out of my mouth were, "Okay, I'll go with you."

It's easy to look back at this conversation forty years later, and see that the hand of God was at work in key points of my life. He had always been there, protecting me during those crazy drug days from the law, from death, from bad guys, and from the car accident. Now these key moments happen: Gloria's faith, her insisting on taking the kids to church, and me being confronted with all this Jesus stuff.

It was during this time that my business was starting to go downhill as the "sure thing" deals started to fall apart. One of the steps along the way on my spiritual journey was a book by Og Mandino, *The Greatest Salesman in the World*. I was told it was a great book to help with sales. This was true, and it inadvertently introduced me to the "sales techniques" of Jesus as He "sold" His message. Curiously enough, reading that book began to soften my bitterness toward Jesus. Growing up, that Name was not mentioned in our home. In fact, as kids, we would use the name when we learned how to curse. Now I am being introduced to Him as the greatest salesman. Step by step, God knew what it would take to get to me.

So, when the kids popped that question about church, I thought, *Okay, I'll go to church; maybe it will be good for business.* So I held my breath, and the next Sunday we went as a family to the Baptist church. When I saw the big cross in the front, I cringed. The cross has always been a hard symbol to look at, as it conjured up images of the persecution of my people that was done in the name of Jesus and with the symbol of a cross. It was turned around and used as a sword throughout the history of our people, from the time of Constantine, to the Crusades, to the Inquisition, the Holocaust, and many other events in between. In some way, I felt like a traitor. *What would my parents or grandparents say if they knew?*

Well, the walls didn't collapse when I walked in, and I didn't get struck by lightning. Since I was fairly well known in the town from my business and community involvement, there were many familiar faces at the church. Everyone was very nice. Little did I know that Gloria had alerted folks that her Jewish husband may be coming, and asked them to be praying. While at the church, I saw Chris and Bonnie Thomas, whom I had previously met. In one of many of Gloria's subtle (or not so subtle) attempts to get me "saved," she once invited these "big guns" of the faith to a barbecue at our house. So when they saw me, they greeted me warmly. Chris invited me to attend a men's Bible study that was for young businessmen in the community. It was held at 6:30 a.m. on Wednesdays.

My first thought was, *That could also be good for business,* so I decided to start attending.

Thus began the next step on my journey: reading the Bible. When I was growing up attending the yeshiva in New York, I learned to read, write, and speak Hebrew. We studied the Torah (the five books of Moses) and commentary as well as some Talmud, which is rabbinic commentary and stories related to the Torah. We also studied Jewish history. But one thing that was completely off limits was the New Testament. I don't know who actually verbalized it, whether at home or at school, but the warning was clear: if you read the New Testament, you would be cursed because it is antisemitic and exhibits hatred toward us.

So here I am, attending a men's Bible study, and we are studying the book of John in the New Testament. This is the first time in my life that I had ever read the New Testament or the words of Jesus. As I attended week after week, I was continually amazed at the Jewishness of the words that we were reading. I knew that Jesus was Jewish, but I never really thought through what that meant. He grew up in Israel in a 1st century Jewish culture. Obviously, His whole family was Jewish. He was called Rabbi, and all His followers were Jewish. He went to synagogue on Shabbat, read from the scrolls of the Torah, and observed all the commands of the Torah. This began to intrigue me.

This is not the picture of the man that I thought of when I heard the name "Jesus." To me, and to most Jews, He is the Christian god, not the God for Jews. They believe that He is a god or something. We Jews believe in one God, as in the Jewish central prayer, the *Shema,* which goes, "Hear, O Israel, the Lord is our God, the Lord is ONE." The idea of Jesus as God would seem to contradict this foundational belief in Judaism, until I came to understand what it meant.

So how did I get from the moment in the AA counselor's office where I reluctantly agreed that there is something outside myself "like a tree" that I could believe in, to this moment of reading about Jesus in the New Testament? How did I become interested in and intrigued by who this person is?

This was now about a year after the "Don't bother me with that Jesus stuff, I'm Jewish," encounter with Gloria. We were still involved in AA and Alanon, and Gloria had re-dedicated her life to God and become a Jesus follower. She was leaving tracts around the house for me to "find," with messages about God and Jesus. She was taking our kids to church. I was going through difficult challenges with the real estate deals that I had gotten into. But beyond all of that, there was now a part of me that was deeply troubled and looking for answers. The Og Mandino book started to soften my attitude toward Jesus and the whole idea of the exis- tence of the God of the Bible ... and now I'm reading the actual New Testament.

The view of God I had held my whole life was that He was dis- tant and uninvolved in the affairs of men. He was certainly not a personal God who cared about me, the way He was now being described to me. Growing up in the Jewish religious culture, my concern was only to fit in, hide the shame of the divorce and Mom's remarriage to a gentile, and pretend to be a religious Jew like the rest of the kids in school. So now my journey was tran- sitioning from atheism, to agnosticism, and now to starting to understand the God of the Bible and Jesus.

By going to the weekly Bible study, I came to realize that Jesus did not come to start a new religion called Christianity. He actually came to call the people of Israel back to a life reflecting what the Torah was meant to be, not what the religious leaders had made it. It was the first time I heard of the concept of God's love—that everything He says and does is out of His love for His people.

CHAPTER 14
STEPPING STONES

I was attending the Bible study regularly as well as the Baptist church with Gloria and the kids when we had them. In addition, I started to read the Bible on my own. The more I read, the more intrigued I became. It was almost like God was putting out a trail of crumbs for me to follow. I started reading the "Old Testament," as well, which is the Hebrew Bible. I came to understand that what Christians call the Old Testament is the same thing as the Hebrew Bible, except that some of the books are arranged differently. The Hebrew Bible is called *TaNaK* in Hebrew, which is an acronym for the three parts of the Bible: the *Torah* (the five books of Moses), the *Neveeim* (the Prophets), and the *Ketuvim* (the Writings, i.e., Psalms, Proverbs and others).

As I began to be immersed in reading the Bible, both the *Tanak* and the *Brit Chadashah* (New Covenant), I began to see the connection between the two. They are actually one book. I learned that all the writers of the New Testament were Jewish, with the possible exception of Luke, but I later learned that there is strong evidence that he was also Jewish. After all, he was a doctor in the community!

At the men's Bible study, there were several of the men there that I knew from the business world in Estes Park, which was a small town where pretty much everyone knew everyone. Chris led the study, and I met a guy, Wayne, who would come to be one of my best friends up till today, nearly forty years later. Wayne was a fellow Jew. He had an interesting story. He was born and raised in New Jersey in a traditional Jewish home. In his twenties, he got caught up in some kind of religious cult in Texas. His parents hired a de-programmer, and they captured him from the group and brought him to his senses. One day he was out hitchhiking and was picked up by Bonnie Thomas' brother, the son of Cliff Barrows. Wayne was aimlessly drifting along at the time, so Bob Barrows recommended that he go see his sister and her husband out in Estes Park at their Bible school there. Wayne made the trip and began to work at the Bible School. In due course, he came to be a follower of Jesus. As a fellow Jew, we bonded pretty quickly, although I was not ready to fully come to believe in my heart that Jesus was the Messiah. However, I was getting close.

We were starting to get involved in the church even beyond Sunday mornings as part of a small group that was building relationships. Gloria would also attend the Sunday evening service at the church. One Sunday evening, she came home after service and was all excited. There had been a guest speaker, named Eliezer Urbach, whom she described as a man with "a long white beard," who "spoke with an accent," and "blew a horn." Eliezer was some kind of missionary in Denver and had a following that called themselves "Messianic."

My response was, "Well, if he believes, in Jesus, he is no longer Jewish." As I reflect on that statement, I realize how silly it was. But that is what I believed at the same, and unfortunately, most Jews believe. The simple truth is that Jewishness is based on ethnicity. I am Jewish because my parents were Jewish, and their parents before them, and so on. Even as an atheist, I was still Jewish. One of my teachers used to say that just like a leopard can't lose its spots, a Jew can never stop being a Jew. It's like saying a Chinese person who believes in Jesus is no longer Chinese. Pretty silly! But that is where I was at that time. Gloria kept his card, which would come in handy later.

As time went on, the business situation continued to get worse. Little did I realize that, while I had made some hasty decisions in my greed to reach my goal of being a millionaire, God was behind the scene. Somehow He was orchestrating events and allowing the situation to deteriorate so that I would eventually take my eyes off the material world and look up. However, things were to get worse before they got better.

Meanwhile, Gloria was more zealous than ever for me to accept Jesus and get saved. She continued leaving tracts around the house, and constantly telling me how I needed to accept Jesus. I would later tell her that if she was the only believer in Jesus that I knew, I might never have come to faith! One time we were standing in the kitchen and a burner was lit. We had a gas stove, and as the flame shot up, she burst out with, "Me and the kids will be floating around in heaven, and you will be burning in hell if you don't accept Jesus!"

I thought, *Oh boy, she's lost it!*

We joke about it now, but at the time, it was definitely a source of tension in the marriage and not a recommended strategy for couples.

While I continued my own journey of reading and studying, people would give me books and pamphlets to read. Two books that got my attention were *The Late, Great, Planet Earth* by Hal Lindsay, and *More Than a Carpenter* by Josh McDowell. In Hal Lindsay's book, he describes so-called "end time" events that are foretold in the Bible. Some have already come to pass, like the return of the Jewish people to the Land, but there are other events that have yet to be fulfilled that all lead up to the return of Jesus. That book really got my attention. The book by Josh McDowell was really helpful because it was based on evidence of the Bible's authenticity and the evidence for the resurrection of Jesus.

So this spiritual journey continued, from atheism to "God, as you understand Him," to reading the Bible, including the New

Testament, to being challenged as to what if He is the Messiah? But how could I trust that He is who He said He is, that He actually existed, and that the stories in this ancient book, the Bible, are real? In *More Than a Carpenter*, a lot of my questions were answered.

I appreciated the fact that the author himself had been an atheist and scoffer of the Bible and is now is an ardent defender of Christianity. In the book, he gives solid evidence of the authenticity of the Bible as compared to other even older writings such as Caesar's *The Gallic Wars*, Homer's *Illiad*, and many others. In some of these ancient writings that scholars believe are authentic, there are no extant copies of the original manuscripts than there are several original scrolls of the Bible.

The other big event, and in fact the most important event in the whole Bible, is the resurrection of Jesus. If the resurrection of Jesus did not take place, then Christianity is all a farce. As C. S. Lewis puts it, "He is either a liar, lunatic, or Lord. He is either who He says He is, or He is a phony and delusional, and has fooled millions of people throughout history." This logic refutes the idea that He was a prophet, a great moral teacher, but not God. But He plainly said He was God and the Messiah. So, He has to be one or the other based on His own words. He is either who He said He was, or he was delusional if he really believed this falsehood, or he knew it was not true and therefore was a liar.

At one time, I would have agreed with the statement that He was a great teacher and prophet, but not God or the Messiah. I was questioning everything. It turns out that there is solid evidence for the resurrection. Evidence is not necessarily the same as proof. Evidence in a court of law is primarily based on witness' accounts and the facts. So there are certain facts that are substantiated and clear. For one, there was absolutely a man who lived 2,000 years ago, and the name we know him by is Jesus, although His Hebrew name—the name his mother gave him—was Yeshua ... more on that later.

There is also ample evidence that He had followers and proclaimed Himself to be the promised Messiah of Israel and the world. There is also evidence that He was crucified by the Romans, that He was buried, and that three days later the tomb was empty. Skeptics have claimed that either 1) He wasn't really dead, or 2) His disciples stole the body. Both of these claims defy logic because 1) the Romans were really efficient at execution by crucifixion, and 2) there was a temple guard or Roman guard assigned to guard the tomb. Moreover, it was highly unlikely that the disciples, who were already traumatized and fearful for their lives, would overpower the guards, steal the body and then claim He had risen. Also take note of the fact that it is recorded in the Bible that He appeared to over 500 people in His resurrected state (I Corinthians 15:6). There is also outside collaboration by Josephus, the Jewish historian who corroborated the report of the disciples.

Having therefore read all the evidence, I was beginning to really be challenged by the idea, *If what I am reading is true, what does that mean for me and my life as a Jewish man?*

Around this time, someone gave me a book about Isaiah 53. (People were always giving me books and pamphlets to read. I knew their motives were pure; they wanted me to know the truth and believe in Jesus.) I read the short book about Isaiah 53; then read it in the Bible, the "Old Testament" part. This part struck me:

He was despised and rejected by men, a man of sorrows, acquainted with grief, One from whom people hide their faces. He was despised, and we did not esteem Him.
Surely He has borne our griefs and carried our pains. Yet we esteemed Him stricken, struck by God, and afflicted.
But He was pierced because of our transgressions, crushed because of our iniquities. The chastisement for our shalom was upon Him, and by His stripes we are healed.
(Isaiah 53:3-5, quoted from Tree of Life translation of Hebrew Scriptures).

As I read this passage, the reality sank in me that here was a man who would suffer and die and take upon Himself the transgressions, sins, iniquities, grief, pain, and sickness of the people. I was dumbfounded. My first thought was, *If any of this is true, this has to be written about the Messiah to come, and it certainly sounds like Jesus based on what I have already read in the men's Bible study on the gospel of John.*

Another step in my faith journey happened at that moment. I came to the intellectual conclusion that Jesus had to be the Messiah, if any of this was true at all. It seemed to me that the evidence was overwhelming. It was getting harder to refute. I now believed, based on evidence, at least intellectually, that the Bible was historically authentic, that Jesus was a real person who lived in Israel in the 1st century, that He started a movement, had devoted followers, and preached about something called the Kingdom of God. The evidence also made it clear that He was crucified, was buried, and the climax of it all was that He rose from the dead, confirming His claim to be the Messiah.

As I began to study more of the writings of the Jewish prophets regarding the Messiah, which have hundreds of references, it became clear that only one person fits the descriptions. I began to see all of this as one big puzzle with lots of pieces that once put together, would emerge as the picture of Jesus, the Messiah, who was promised to the Jewish people throughout the Hebrew Scripture.

I can remember when I was growing up, my maternal grandmother would often say things like, "When the *Mashiach* (Messiah) comes ..." with the general implication that He would fix things and the world would be at peace. I always thought that was a *bubba meiser*, a Yiddish expression kind of like an "old wives' tale," literally meaning "grandma's story." In reality, the idea of a Messiah coming has been ingrained in the Jewish psyche for thousands of years, and most today are still waiting for Him.

Could Jesus, the one who was the cause of all the years of hatred and persecution, or so I thought, *could He actually be the promised Messiah? If so, what does that mean for me at this point in my life?*

With all these questions in my mind, I continued to attend the Bible study, church, and small group. I was also reading and studying both the Old and New Testaments on my own. The more I read, the more I began to realize how truly Jewish the New Testament is, especially the four gospels. Each one gives a slightly different account of Jesus' life and ministry. I knew He was Jewish, but I never realized how Jewish He really was. He followed all of the Torah, and never taught anything contrary. All His followers were Jewish, and they never stopped being Jewish. They went to synagogue on Shabbat and observed all the Jewish feasts and festivals. There was never a question about His or His followers' Jewishness. He didn't start a new religion called Christianity. They were the Nazarenes, or followers of the man from Nazareth, and were another sect among the many others in Israel in the 1st century.

In August, 1984, my dad came out to visit us in Estes Park, which he did pretty often. That week, on a Wednesday morning at 6:00 I got up to go to the men's Bible study. My dad was up too. "What are you doing up so early?" he asked.

So I told him, "I go to a men's Bible study on Wednesdays with a group of young businessmen in town."

"Why is a Jewish guy like you going to a Bible study?"

"I am just learning," I replied.

By the look on his face, I could tell he was clearly not happy. I had not told him anything about my recent spiritual journey, knowing that he would not approve. The conversation was over at that point, but a few days later, as I was taking him to the airport to return to New York, he asked me point blank, "Are you involved in Christianity?"

"I'm looking into it," I replied.

"Don't let Gloria influence you; don't forget you're Jewish."

"It has nothing to do with Gloria—I am just learning and, of course, I would never forget the fact that I'm Jewish."

I could tell Dad was agitated, and, honestly, I understood why. I can imagine he was remembering the Holocaust and the persecutions of the Jewish people by "so- called" Christians. As I recalled the conversation with Dad, I remembered the horrors of the death camps from the photos I'd seen in his drawer. I would look at them when he wasn't around, but I never asked him about the subject. Now, I wish I had. I often wondered if he had seen the camps first-hand during his army time; hence the photos.

The rest of the ride to the airport was fairly quiet.

Despite my father's disapproval, I continued going to the men's Bible study and growing in my understanding and relationship with God. My friendship with Wayne was also developing. At the same time, our finances got worse, and we were forced to give up the "yellow" house. The day we moved, Wayne came and helped us. He brought with him Tom Trento, a guy who had spoken at our Bible study. Tom had a ministry in Denver specializing in "apologetics." I connected with Tom, who came from New Jersey—a very down to earth Italian family.

What is apologetics? I learned that it is the ability to defend your faith based on the evidence from the Bible, to be able to explain logically why the Bible is real, why God exists, and, most importantly, the evidence of the resurrection of Yeshua. So Wayne brings Tom along to help me move, and I find out later that he told Tom that I was not yet a believer but needed help.

My meeting with Tom Trento will become a significant moment in our story later on.

CHAPTER 15
YOM KIPPUR, 1984

It was the fall of 1984. I was conflicted in my heart because, on the one hand, I intellectually believed that Jesus must be the Messiah, but I was also still having trouble with the whole Christianity thing and feeling like a traitor to my people. I still went to church every Sunday, Bible study on Wednesdays, and met up with my small group from church mid-week. Ironically, through all this, I was still running away from God. But it gave me time to think through all the things I was hearing.

As the Fall Holy Days of the Jewish calendar were approaching, I began to think that maybe I needed to get back in touch with my Jewish roots. What would be the best way to do that? The only thing I could think of was to go to synagogue.

The Fall Holy Days is a time when Jewish people all over the world gather at synagogue. Judaism has its own calendar consisting of twelve lunar months, each month lasting 30 days. There are three main fall feasts or holy days. The first is *Rosh Hashanah*, the Feast of Trumpets, which literally is the start of the new Jewish year. Ten days after Rosh Hashanah is *Yom Kippur*, the Day of Atonement, considered the holiest day of the Jewish calendar. The overall theme of these days is repentance and asking for forgiveness for the sins committed in the prior year with the hope of being "inscribed in the book of life" for another year. The falls feasts culminate in *Sukkot*, or the Feast of Tabernacles, which is celebrated for eight days to commemorate the time that the Israelites lived in tents in the wilderness and utterly depended on God for provision.

Jewish people who don't go to synagogue any other time of the year will usually go during these days. It is kind of like Christians who only go to church on Christmas and Easter. This describes around 85-90 percent of the Jewish people in the U.S. who are mostly secular. The remaining 10-15 percent are orthodox, meaning that they follow all the rabbinic laws and observances of the Sabbath and the Holy Days, and attend synagogue regularly throughout the year.

So here I am, a Jew going to church and Bible study, and feeling a bit like a traitor. Now I was going to synagogue for the Holy Days. There was one catch, though: money. I remembered that going to synagogue during the high Holy Days required purchasing tickets. Now I was remembering the shame that I associated this with when I was a kid. We would go to synagogue every Shabbat, and be able to sit wherever we chose, as it was not very crowded. I was even in the choir for a time, so I got to sit close to the front on the side of the bimah (platform). However, when it came to the Holy Days, we could only afford the least expensive tickets, and we would be in the last couple of rows, along with the people who only attended once a year and could not afford better seats. This was more embarrassment and shame for me.

As I was thinking about this, I remembered the Messianic congregation that the guy who came to the church had told Gloria about. I wondered if they charged for tickets. So I asked Gloria, "Hey, do you still have that guy's card that came to the church and told you about that congregation in Denver?"

The answer was "Yes, right here!" and she handed me the card.

So, I called the number, and Eliezer answered the phone, sounding kind of grumpy, like I'd woken him up.

"Is this Eliezer?" I asked.

"Yes, who is this?"

"My name is Ira; you met my wife at the First Baptist Church in Estes Park."

"Yes, okay, so?"

"I was calling to see if you had services for Yom Kippur and if you charge for tickets."

"Yes, we have service for Yom Kippur, and no, we don't charge—just come," was his reply.

I got the address in Denver where they met, which was ironically in the basement of another Baptist church. This was a few days before Yom Kippur, and so we made plans to go on *Erev Yom Kippur* (the night of Yom Kippur). At this time, Judy and her husband Ron had moved to Longmont, which is about thirty miles from Estes Park, and the kids were living with them, making it harder for us to get them. But we still got them when we could. Sammi was ten and Seth was eight. So we arranged to go to Denver the evening of Yom Kippur and pick up Sammi along the way. Another friend from the Bible school also came along with us.

So we got to the location of the service, in the basement of that Baptist church. As I walked in, I knew I was home.

I was greeted by a young man at the door, who I later found out was Eliezer's son, Chaim. He and I would become lasting friends. Sadly, he recently passed away. Even though we were in the basement of a Baptist church, I felt like it was a synagogue. The men were wearing prayer shawls and *kippahs* (caps), and there was Jewish sounding music playing and a replica of the ark that contained a Torah scroll. At this moment, I sensed God saying to me, "See, you're not the only one," meaning I'm not the only Jew to believe in Jesus. In fact, I heard the name "Yeshua" for the first time.

Now it was all coming together, and I no longer felt conflicted about believing in Jesus. From this point on, I would call Him *Yeshua*, the name His mother gave Him. It made more sense now, recalling the verse in the gospel where the angel comes to Joseph and tells him, "You will call His name Jesus, for he will save His people from their sin." Looking at the original Hebrew, it would have been, "You shall call His name Yeshua (which means salvation), for He will save His people from their sin."

During the Yom Kippur service, there is a very traditional and somber prayer that is chanted at the start of the service called *Kol Nidre*, which means "All our Vows." It is a disavowal of vows that were made under duress during the past year. It goes back to the time when Jews were persecuted and forced to renounce Judaism and be baptized or face death. Since life in the Jewish understanding of it is to be valued above all things, vows were often made under duress in order to preserve life. This prayer is thought to go back to the time of the Spanish Inquisition, when Jews were forced at the point of a sword to renounce their Jewish faith and convert to Christianity. Since Yom Kippur is the one day of the year that traditionally we are to seek God for forgiveness for the sins of the past year, the Kol Nidre prayer expresses that desire.

It is the day that in the Torah, the high priest is the one who comes to God and seeks forgiveness on behalf of the people. He has to offer a sacrifice for himself and his family, so he is free of sin before he enters into the Holy of Holies and makes atonement on behalf of the whole nation. This is done with the "scapegoat." The high priest lays his hands on the head of the goat, confesses the sins of the nation, and then God in His mercy, allows the symbolic transfer of the sin of the nation to the goat; the goat is then sent out into the wilderness to a cliff and fall to its death. I saw that night that Yeshua fulfilled both the roles of the High Priest, and of the sacrifice. In both roles, they were eternal: Jesus did it once for all time, not year after year, as prescribed in the Torah.

In synagogue services traditionally there is a cantor, a gifted singer that is trained in the chanting of the prayers that are recited on Shabbat and the Holy Days, and a rabbi who delivers a sermon.

Tonight, on this Yom Kippur, at my first Messianic service, there was a cantor by the name of Bill Berg, who chanted the Kol Nidre prayer. There was beautiful music and song that had a distinctly Jewish sound, unlike the Baptist hymns at the church I attended with Gloria. Gloria cried the whole time, saying the music "ministered to my soul."

My heart was also deeply touched, and it all was beginning to make sense. I was starting to be at peace with the idea that I could believe in Yeshua, the Jewish Messiah, and still be Jewish. The fact is that I now saw how much believing in Yeshua had made my Jewishness more meaningful. I began to see how silly the notion is that those two realities would be in conflict.

The message that night was given by Burt Yellin, who from what I understood, had submitted his application to be the rabbi. After the service, I finally met Eliezer and his wife, Sara. They were with an organization called the American Board of Mission to the Jews (ABMJ), an organization that has been around for about a hundred years, and is dedicated to sharing the love of Yeshua with Jewish people. Little did I know how connecting with these people that night would impact my life for years to come.

After the service, we got in the car to head home. First, we dropped off Sammi in Longmont; then we headed up the mountain back to Estes Park. Gloria and our friend were chatting about the service and whatever else. I was in my own zone. There was a particular spot along the road leading up to Estes Park when you drove out of the canyon type road into an open area called Meadowdale. Along the way, I was thinking about what I'd just experienced in the Yom Kippur service, and processing all that I'd learned over the prior two years.

As I was contemplating all of this in my heart, I just surrendered, and at that moment, an incredible sense of peace came over me. I knew that at this moment I was experiencing the very presence of God. In my heart I said, "Yes, Yeshua, come into my heart,

I know that You are the promised Messiah who died for my sins that I might truly experience the atonement of this night." I didn't say a word, but I knew that something dramatic and life-changing had just occurred. Another big step in my journey!

We dropped our friend off, and when we got home, I told Gloria, "I did it!"

"You did what?" she asked.

"I received Yeshua into my heart," I declared.

"Where was I?"

"You were in the car talking to Mary. We were coming up to Meadowdale, and I just surrendered to Yeshua and received Him into my heart. I felt His peace for the first time."

Gloria was so surprised, "I thought there would be lightning or the sky would light up when you came to faith."

"Well, it did for me."

It was years later that I learned the details of my mom and her family's escape from Berlin. The "rendezvous in Paris" happened on Yom Kippur forty-seven years earlier!

For me, it was another major step in my journey, and it would change everything, which I didn't know at the time. One of my first thoughts was, *Okay God, now that I have fully surrendered to You, You are going to fix my financial mess, right?* The answer to that question I was soon to learn was a resounding "NO!" The reason was not because God was mean or stingy, but because He was literally changing the course of my life. I was not the same person that I thought I was. Little did I know at the time that He was remaking me and redirecting my path.

We continued to attend the Baptist church, and every few weeks on Shabbat, we would drive down to Denver to attend the service at Roeh Israel, the Messianic congregation that held the Yom Kippur service. During these visits, we were getting to know Eliezer and his wife Sara, their son Chaim, and the new rabbi of the congregation, Burt. After service, Eliezer would invite us to their home for lunch, and he would answer all my questions about what it meant to be a Jew who believes in Yeshua, questions like, "What about the Torah? Does it still apply for today? What does it mean to be a Jewish believer in Yeshua? How is it different than being a Christian?" and more.

During this time, our finances were going from bad to worse. Neither of the two big development deals that I was working on came through. I had put my hopes of financial success into these two projects, and they both fell apart for various reasons, leaving me deeply in debt and devastated. We lost our dream house and had to rent an apartment in a duplex in Estes Park. However, inspite of these difficulties, God was molding and shaping me into the person that He designed me to be.

FINAL WORDS WITH DAD

One Saturday afternoon in November 1984, we came home from spending the day in Denver attending the congregation and having lunch with Eliezer and Sara. There was a note on the door to call Janet, my secretary from the office, saying it was urgent. The news was not good. My dad had a sudden heart attack and died at home.

He was there by himself when he had the heart attack. Dad had suffered from heart issues for as long as I could remember. He had a couple of surgeries, and he battled with his weight. His upbringing in Vienna with rich foods that he liked his whole life most likely contributed to his condition. He was one month shy of his sixty-sixth birthday. It was a terrible shock, and we made plans to get Sammi and Seth and head to NY for the funeral and to sit *shiva*, the traditional mourning time.

A couple of weeks after the Yom Kippur night, when I gave my heart to Yeshua, I felt led to write my dad and ask for his forgiveness. I knew I had disappointed him by dropping out of college, wasting his money that he would send me, and also that I had borrowed money from him and couldn't repay it. I wrote this letter asking him to forgive me. He called me right away and thanked me and forgave me. I know that God led me to write that letter, so that when a few weeks later he was gone, I could at least be comforted in knowing that I had asked for his forgiveness and felt at peace.

We all went up for the funeral and sitting shiva (one week of mourning according to Jewish tradition). I was very young in the faith and struggled to reconcile my new faith in Yeshua with the Jewish traditions of funerals and mourning. I have since come to see that there is great wisdom in the Jewish tradition of mourning, where you disconnect from everything for a week (*shiva* comes from the Hebrew word *sheva* for number seven), then 30 days where you go back to work, but still in mourning; then finally eleven month, the official end of the mourning period with the unveiling of the headstone.

Dad and Maya had previously purchased a home on a lake in Sagamore, NY, upstate from the city. They would go up on weekends and holidays. We had been there and enjoyed vacations, even when I was still married to Judy, and Sammi and Seth were little.

IMMERSION

On one of our Saturday afternoon lunches with Eliezer and Sara, Eliezer talked to me about water baptism. That was the last thing that I wanted to do. After all, that is so "Christian," and it would be the final betrayal of being Jewish. How could I do that? However, Eliezer explained to me that baptism, while seemingly a "Christian thing," is actually quite Jewish. The word "baptism" comes from a Greek word *baptismo* that simply means "immerse." The original immersion practice or ritual comes from the time when the priests and Levites that came to minister in the Temple in Jerusalem went through the *mikveh*, or ritual bath, as a sign of purification before they could come into the Temple and offer the sacrifices on behalf of the people. From that ritual, came the immersion of John the Baptist, an immersion of repentance.

So when I understood that as a follower of Yeshua, I was to be immersed as a public demonstration of my commitment to Him, I was willing. Under one condition: I would only be immersed if Eliezer would do it. So we contacted Pastor Mike at the Baptist church in Estes Park. He had been very supportive and patient with me in my journey, and the church supported Eliezer financially, so he was very excited about my decision to follow Yeshua. He was more than happy to have Eliezer come up on a Sunday night to speak and to immerse me in the immersion pool at the church. And so, in April 1985, I was immersed publicly at the Baptist church in Estes Park.

CHAPTER 16
THE GREAT RESET

In the summer of 1984, we received the great news that Gloria was pregnant with our second child. This was a surprise since we did not think she could get pregnant again, which is common after abortion. There were a couple of tense moments during the pregnancy when Gloria had some spotting. However, as we were preparing for the birth, which we wanted to go through naturally, we asked Wayne, who had some EMT training, if he would assist in the delivery. Josie Rae was born after a long labor, and we made Wayne her godfather. This was, of course, before sonograms, and we thought she was going to be a boy, in which case we were going to name her after my dad, Joseph. When we were surprised by a girl, we still named her after Dad—Josie.

During our Actualization days we became friends with Michael Bloom (not his real name) who was a secular Jew and had a real estate company in Colorado Springs, about an hour south of Denver. We kept in touch with him, and he attended our wedding. On several occasions, he would tell me that if I ever wanted to leave Estes Park, I could make a lot of money in real estate working for him. At first, I was not interested. After all, in my mind, I was going to strike it rich in Estes with the two development deals I had been working on. However, as things got progressively worse, his offer sounded more and more attractive. So we made plans to move in April 1985 to go to work for Michael, thinking that would solve all my financial problems. Dad had left my brother and me some life insurance, so we had some money to make the move and rent a house in Colorado Springs.

I went to work for Michael, and I thought, "Okay, now I am working real estate in a city, for an established company." However, it did not take long to see that nearly everything that Michael had promised turned out to be false. In fact, the more we got to know him, the more we realized that he was really unscrupulous in the way he ran the business, and he had a very small office. This was unsettling to me since, even before I came to believe in Yeshua, I always ran my business ethically and honestly.

It came to a point where I could no longer work for Michael. I had met another broker in town, and he offered me a position selling commercial real estate. His was a well-respected company in town, and I thought I could make it in this company. However, God had other plans for me, which began to unfold pretty soon.

I continued to run regularly after our move to Colorado Springs. One morning while on a run, I came to an overlook to the mountains. I stopped there to catch my breath, and in this moment I cried out to God, "What are You doing? We moved here to have a better life, but it's worse now!" Of course, I was thinking of everything in terms of our financial situation, which did go from bad to worse. The money from Dad's life insurance was running out, and even in this new company, nothing was happening. I had not closed a single deal, even though I had several seemingly good prospects.

At that moment on that overlook, I heard God say, "It is because I am redirecting your life."

That is all I heard, but in my limited understanding of how God speaks, I realized that He was closing the door to what I thought was my only source of income, real estate. I did not realize it at the time, but this was part of my identity, albeit a false one wrapped up in pride and self-centeredness. God was beginning the process of stripping away that old identity, so that He could re-form me in His image. This was a painful but necessary process. I did not understand it all, but I got the message enough to know that I was no longer that real estate guy.

I promptly resigned my position with the company and embarked on another sales job at an up-and-coming electronic credit card processing company. It entailed selling point-of-sale units and signing retail companies up for electronic processing. It started out pretty well, but then I hit a wall. The company was sold, and I was let go. Our economic situation kept getting worse. Gloria started cleaning houses for work, which helped, and I was at a loss what to do next. At this point, I think the only thing I knew to do to make money was sales. But apparently, I was not very good at it.

MARRIAGE GOD'S WAY

As a result of the financial pressure, we were also having problems in the marriage, even to the point where my mom told Gloria she should leave me and go back to Mississippi to her parents. Thankfully, she did not listen to that advice. Instead, we found a Christian counselor, who offered help on a free-will offering basis. When we sat down with the counselor, he opened the Bible and read to us the roles for the husband and the wife that were spelled out in scripture. This was the first time we had read these words.

"Husbands love your wives as Messiah loved the church and gave Himself up for her..."(Ephesians 5:25) *Wow, that's my role!* Loving her meant doing whatever it took to help her feel safe and secure, and to sacrifice for her, as Yeshua did for us.

"Wives, respect your husbands and submit to their authority..." (Ephesians 5:22). That was a wow for Gloria as well. It put the burden of leadership on me, to provide, to protect, and to care for. Her role was to "submit" and "to come alongside and walk together."

We realized that we were in this together and needed to work as a team. This was a real turning point for me and for us as a couple. From that moment on, I came to the place where I was willing to do anything to provide, even if it meant delivering pizzas. I literally started looking in the newspaper for jobs.

NEW CONNECTIONS

At this time, we were going to a newly-formed church led by a couple of young pastors in Colorado Springs. We met a couple in the church; the husband was a Jewish believer, young in the Lord like me, and the wife was a Gentile. She was the HR director at an NCR (National Cash Register) chip manufacturing plant that was in Colorado Springs, and she was able to get me a job working in the plant, in a clean room, working the graveyard shift. This began a wonderful chapter of learning the discipline of a "real" job. I had been accustomed to working for myself, setting my own hours, and being my own boss, but God used this job as another step in my spiritual growth.

When we told Eliezer that we were moving to Colorado Springs, he asked me if I would help him get speaking engagements in churches in the town. He had always wanted to extend his speaking opportunities to share about Israel and the importance of Christians sharing the love of Yeshua with Jewish people. He gave me a script and a list of churches, and so I was happy to help him. Cold calling for this purpose was no big deal for me. I was able to get him several speaking engagements in churches. These typically were on a Sunday night, and he and Sara would come down to the Springs from Denver, stay with us, and we would accompany them to the church. In this way, I was getting some on-the-job training that would be helpful down the road, as well as learning the importance of hospitality. At this time, I was just helping him out, not knowing what God had ahead for us.

Eliezer introduced us to several folks he knew in the Springs that were interested in Jewish outreach and living Jewish lives as believers. Some were Jewish, and some non-Jewish. One couple that we became very close to was Monte and Lin. Monte was a really smart guy, who knew the Bible well, and he became a mentor for me. They knew our struggles and were a source of support and encouragement. The group of us began to meet on Friday nights for Shabbat. We would usher in the Shabbat with traditional candle lighting, wine—grape juice in our case—and *challah*, the special braided loaf that is traditional for Shabbat.

During this time, we were learning what it meant to live a Jewish life in Messiah. Although I was raised Jewish, in the yeshiva, going to the Orthodox synagogue, I really did not know the "whys" of many things that we did. It seems that now, as a believer in Yeshua as the Messiah, I was for the first time understanding the calling and purpose of the Jewish people and what it meant to be the "chosen" people. As Tevya in *Fiddler on the Roof* would famously say in his *kvetching* (complaining) to God, "I know You've chosen us, but could You choose someone else for a change?" In other words, for many Jewish people, being "chosen" meant being singled out for hatred, persecution, and murder, throughout history. But I was learning that we were actually chosen for a different reason.

The meetings on Friday night grew as we met other folks who were interested in learning about living a Jewish life as believers in Yeshua. These were both Jewish and non-Jewish people. I was learning that there is a great interest among Christians to learn about the Jewish roots of the faith. Historically, Jewish influence in the believers in the faith was stomped out. I came to understand that there was a deep, ingrained anti-Jewish bias in much of church theology that goes back to the 2nd century. At that time, the first followers of Yeshua were all Jewish, and so were the leaders of the now growing community of believers in Israel. The apostles, for example, and their disciples were all Jewish, and it never occurred to them that faith in the Jewish Messiah now constituted conversion to a different religion. To them there was no question of not living as Jews.

However, as the gospel spread throughout the Roman world into all the major cities by Paul and his team, many Gentiles came to believe in the Jewish Messiah. Though many were coming out of paganism, in some cases, many were already worshiping the God of Israel and attending synagogue as proselytes. Such Gentiles were called "God-fearers." When they heard the good news of the Messiah, and especially upon learning that they did not have to be circumcised in order to be considered full members of this new community of faith, more Gentiles came in droves directly out of paganism.

FROM SHABBAT TO SUNGOD DAY

However, as the gospel spread over the next two centuries, eventually Christianity went from being a persecuted faith to an institutionalized religion. Under the Emperor Constantine, it became the official religion of the Roman Empire. Along with that decree, came the purging of any Jewish practices in the churches. An early doctrine of this emerging religion was that the destruction of the second Temple was evidence that God had rejected the Jewish people, and thus they were cursed. Therefore, it made sense to eradicate any Jewish elements from the practice of Christianity.

Therein lies the beginning of the so-called "replacement theology" that still exists today in much of Christian theology. Removed from this new state religion were practices like circumcision, keeping of kosher laws, observance of Shabbat, and the Jewish feast days. Instead, the Sabbath was changed from Saturday to Sunday, the day pagans worshiped the sun god, Mithra. Passover was replaced by Easter, the festival day of the fertility goddess, Ishtar. What is even worse, Jewish believers had to prove their faith by eating pork, and renouncing any of the Jewish practices they were commanded to observe in the Torah. All of this was based on the lie that God had rejected the Jewish people as a result of the destruction of the second Temple in Jerusalem in 70 AD by the Romans. Since the leadership of the Jewish people had rejected Jesus as the Messiah, all the Jewish people were blamed for His death and henceforth called "Christ killers." Jews who believed in Yeshua were either forced to renounce their Jewishness or their faith in Yeshua so as to be able to return to the synagogues. Jews who believed in Yeshua while maintaining their practices and following the Torah were considered heretics.

Thus the stage was set for the next 2,000 years of persecution and slaughter of Jewish people in the name of Christ, from the Crusaders, who went through Jewish towns slaughtering the inhabitants, to the Spanish Inquisition, to the pogroms in Russia, and finally to the Holocaust. Hitler claimed to be a Christian, and so did the German soldiers responsible for the gas chambers. Most Jewish people believe that it was Christians that did all these horrible things to us over history; therefore, it is a betrayal for a Jew to become one.

However, I came to understand that not everyone who calls himself a Christian truly is one. The word "Christian" comes from the Greek word *Christianos*, which means "follower of Christ." To be a follower means that you do what that person taught and did. Obviously, the people who persecuted and murdered Jewish people throughout history in His name were not followers of His teachings, but used His name for their own evil agenda. I also learned that the word *Christ* which growing up we used as a curse word, means "Anointed One" in Greek, just as the word "Messiah" comes from the Hebrew word *Mashiach* also means, "Anointed One." Yet, to the average Jewish person, Christ is for Christians, or Gentiles, while Messiah is Jewish. How things have gotten twisted through the misuse of words!

A MESSIANIC CONGREGATION

As our group continued to grow, we began to sense that God was leading us to form a congregation of our own. We were beginning to learn that there is actually a growing "Messianic movement," a movement of Jewish followers of Yeshua who were now forming their own congregations. This movement started in the mid-1960s, as we learned, although throughout history there was always a remnant of Jewish people who believed, aside from those forced to convert or die.

We came across a manuscript of a not-yet-published book by Dan Juster called *Jewish Roots*. This would become a great help to us in forming a theological basis for a Messianic congregation and our understanding of what it means to live a Jewish life as followers of Yeshua. This and other books by Dan, one of the fathers of the modern Messianic movement, would greatly impact me in the formation of a foundation in theology and practice going forward. I also developed a personal relationship with Dan that would take us on some twists and turns over the next thirty-five years.

As we developed the plan to start the congregation, we sought the counsel of Eliezer, Burt, and Chaim, who were the leaders of Roeh Israel, the congregation in Denver. With their guidance, in 1986 we officially formed Congregation Sha'arit Yisrael (Remnant of Israel). Bill Berg, the cantor who chanted the Kol Nidre that Yom Kippur night when I first came to faith, was ordained as a rabbi. I was asked to be an elder, along with Monte Judah. So we were the leaders of the congregation. Looking back, how was it that I could become an elder of the congregation after only being a believer in Yeshua for a couple of years? If not for the guidance, counsel, and encouragement of the mentors in my life at that time, it would not have been possible to succeed in that role. I believe that God was fast tracking me and continuing the process of remaking me into

His image. I can look back on it now and see that He was preparing me for my unfolding destiny.

As time went on, we began to pray about it and believe that we were to go into full-time ministry. Having no idea what that actually meant, I sat down with Eliezer and sought further guidance. He confirmed that what I was sensing was indeed from God. He recognized something in me and recommended that I follow the path of working with the organization that he was a part of, the American Board of Missions to the Jews (ABMJ, later called Chosen People Ministries).

The first step would require me to go to Bible school, specifically Moody Bible Institute in Chicago, which has a Jewish Studies department led by well-known professor and Bible scholar, Dr. Louis Goldberg. There was one catch though as I perused the application process. They had strict guidelines, and one of the rules was that divorced people could not be allowed to be students—so that excluded me!

Around the same time, our fledgling congregation was contacted by the Union of Messianic Jewish Congregations (UMJC), and we were invited to attend a southwest conference in New Mexico at a mountain retreat center called Glorietta. The UMJC is an amalgam of Messianic congregations that was formed a few years earlier by Dan Juster and a few other leaders of congregations. There had been a long-time organization of Jewish believers called the Messianic Jewish Alliance of America that consisted of individuals. It was originally formed in the early 1900s as the Christian Jewish Alliance, and was part of the International Christian Jewish Alliance.

While attending the conference, we met several other Messianic leaders and elders in the southwest area who would become life-long friends. One of the couples we met, who would become mentors and close friends to us was Marty and Marlene Waldman. They had planted and led a congregation in Dallas, Texas. We happened to run into them while we were walking along a path and suddenly looked up, and there they were, sitting on the patio of their cabin. As we waved to them, they invited us to come up and visit.

It turned out that Marty had worked with ABMJ for several years before starting the congregation. Marty and I had a lot in common. His parents were Holocaust survivors, he was raised in a traditional Jewish home too, and he had also been a hippie and druggie. We hit it off immediately and have been close friends ever since. He gave us some advice that would help us make a course correction in the direction that we believed God was leading us. His input was to think and pray about planting a Messianic congregation, rather than go with a missions organization. This immediately resonated with us, as the door to Moody was shut. Also, in my heart, I knew that for me, being in a Messianic congregation was life-changing, as it would be for other Jewish people who were also seekers. We settled that this was the direction that we were to go—to start a Messianic congregation. But where or how was not clear.

At this point, I was still working at the microelectronics plant. I had moved from night to day shift while Gloria was still cleaning houses. We were seeing Sammi and Seth about every other weekend and enjoying being parents to Josie. We knew pretty early on in this process that we would not be staying in Colorado Springs to start another congregation, but that we were to go where there was a large Jewish population. That, in my mind, meant New York or California.

CHAPTER 17
BACK TO SCHOOL

At the time, the UMJC had a program for the training of Messianic rabbis. I enrolled in the program called the Yeshiva Institute. It was designed for students to be able to continue with their normal routine but attend a week of intensive classes and follow up with their research papers that would be sent to the professors. The classes were to take place at different locations twice a year. It was in those classes that I built relationships both with fellow students and with the professors. Typically, the classes were small, with around fifteen to twenty students, and we ate, slept, and hung out together for the week.

One of the yeshiva sessions was in a monastery near Tampa, Florida. It was winter, and I thought, "Yay, a winter break from the cold and snow of Colorado to enjoy Florida!" It turned out the weather was miserable, the place we stayed at had no heat, was cold, rainy, and damp, and I was miserable during the week. However, I met a man who was taking the classes, and that would prove to be another one of those pivotal relationships that would affect our destiny.

Jim Cumiford had been a Christian pastor of sorts when he heard about the classes at this monastery in Tampa. He lived in West Palm Beach. He had a growing interest in the Messianic movement and felt drawn to attend. We spent a good bit of time together, though he unexpectedly left in the middle of the week, saying he was not feeling well. We kept in touch after the week, and he eventually told me thathe felt that God had told him to go to the classes because he was going to meet someone there who would be a key to planting a Messianic congregation in his part of south Florida.

I knew little about Florida then in terms of being a center of Jewish life. I knew that Miami once had a large Jewish population, and that my grandparents used to go down to Miami Beach for vacations, along with many older Jewish people. I learned from Jim that in Palm Beach County, where West Palm Beach was located, there was a growing Jewish population, but there were no Messianic congregations there. As for us, we were not thinking about Florida as a possible location to move; we were thinking more of New York or California, where the two largest Jewish populations are concentrated. So we purposed in our hearts to pray, to seek counsel from our "wise mentors," and to consider the move to Florida.

That year, in 1989, our second daughter was born. Again, we were expecting a boy, and had the name Micah picked out. Lo and behold, it was another girl, so we stuck with the name, just using the transliterated Hebrew, Micha. We gave her the middle name of Gabrielle, after my maternal grandfather, Gabriel, who had passed a few years earlier.

The more we talked about it and sought counsel, the more we felt Florida was where we were to go. So we decided to go on an exploratory trip—"spying out the land," as it were. We flew down to West Palm Beach and met with Jim and his wife and a small group of friends that were part of a church that had a small Messianic fellowship but was looking to start a new congregation. While we were there for the week, we met a Jewish young lady with whom we shared Yeshua's love; she received salvation, and we ended up immersing her in water as well. We believed that this was confirmation that God was indeed leading us to move our family to south Florida for the purpose of leading a Messianic congregation. It would start with this small group. They wanted me to be their Rabbi. After the visit, which was in January 1990, we made plans to move to Florida.

Looking back on the five years we spent in Colorado Springs, they were definitely years filled with challenges and difficulties, but also great blessings. God was remolding and reshaping me to be more and more like Yeshua. Little did I know what the purpose of these challenges would be. But a verse in Proverbs says, "For the Lord disciplines those He loves, as a father the son he delights in" (Proverbs 3:12). The more the difficulties in this time, the more I was driven to Him.

I was spending a lot of time studying His Word. I found a men's Bible study that met on Wednesday mornings with a guy named Bud Accord, who had been a missionary in Africa. He was a great Bible teacher. I as well as the others in the group, learned an incredible amount from him, and felt I was growing exponentially. I think we spent about a year just on Romans 8. The key verse for me was verse 28, "God works all things together for the good of those that love Him and are called according to His purpose." It had never occurred to me that I was "called according to His purpose." Could it be that, through all the hurt, pain, bad decisions, near death experiences, drug abuse, and all the rest, God had a definite purpose for me all along?

Things were starting to make sense, and I was getting an education beyond the college and yeshiva programs. This "education" was orchestrated by the One who knew me and loved me even in my lost and broken state when I was deceived into thinking I was in control of my life. This education was preparing me for what was to be the destiny that He had for me all along, which was to represent Him and His kingdom.

While I was taking the courses for ordination in the yeshiva program, I was also enrolled in a program at Colorado Christian University, which was based in Denver with a branch in Colorado

Springs. Twenty years earlier, I had dropped out of the University of Wisconsin, having only completed three semesters. My grades were not great, but I did pass all my courses. The program at CCU allowed me to apply all my previous credits, including credits from certain real estate classes I'd taken and credits for writing life learning papers on certain topics. The program was for a Bachelor's degree in Human Resource Management. So in the same year, I received a bachelor's degree twenty years after dropping out of college, as well as completed the necessary courses for an ordination as a Messianic Rabbi.

After the visit to Florida in January 1990, we made plans to move there. We did not own our own home, and we were living on short-term rentals. One Shabbat at the congregation, we got to know the Silverbergs, who had recently moved to Colorado Springs from south Florida. They offered to share the cost of shipping the furniture with us if we wanted to load our stuff on their trailer. Even though we knew we weren't going to be moving for a couple of months, we thought this was a good opportunity to move our furniture and belongings at a reasonable price.

At this point, the plan was to relocate to West Palm Beach and connect with the group that we had met on our visit. However, as time went by, we began to wonder if this was the right group to come in and lead. Bill and Mary, the leaders at the time, were in touch with us. As it got closer to the time to move, we sensed that there was a certain element of control they seemed to be asserting as to how things were to go forward with us coming down. Although we were pretty naive at this stage, we were having second thoughts about whether this was the best connection for us. We were confident that God was calling us to South Florida, but was this the right association for us? It turned out that God definitely had different plans for us.

Folks from the group offered to rent a truck and drive down to pick up our stuff when it came off the train in Pompano Beach, about an hour south of where they were. Arrangements were made for our stuff to be picked up and loaded into the U-Haul and put our stuff in storage in West Palm Beach to await our arrival a couple of months later. On the way down to pick up our stuff, their U-Haul broke down, and they never got there. However, the Silverbergs had a friend who owned a storage facility, and they made arrangements to store our things there.

When we heard about this, we were not sure what to do. But, stepping back, we realized that this was the hand of God protecting us and re-directing us to places we didn't know at the time.

OPERATION RESCUE

Once I became a believer in Yeshua, my views on moral issues began to change as well. One major change was my view of abortion. As believers in Yeshua now, both Gloria and I had deep regrets about the abortion that we had, realizing that we had killed our baby. But we also knew that we had God's forgiveness, and we wanted to use our experience to encourage others and help prevent them from making the same mistake.

We were hearing about the pro-life movement for the first time. It had been gaining momentum since the Rowe v. Wade decision to legalize abortion in 1973. At the time I thought that was a great decision. I had bought the lie that it was a woman's right to choose—"My body, my choice!" But the truth is that the baby has a separate body. So it was no longer the mother's body and the mother's rights they were defending. We now realized this was a deception.

There was an active pro-life movement in Denver, and we jumped in. They were planning a sit-in to block an abortion clinic in Denver and a rally at a church. Because Gloria was pregnant with Micha, it was not wise for her to participate in the sit-in, but she was asked to speak at the church rally as someone who had experienced an abortion. At the sit-in, we blocked the entrance to the abortion clinic. The forty of us protestors all got arrested and taken to the jail in Denver. This is now the second time I had been arrested and spent a night in jail, although this time for a noble cause. We all got charged with trespassing and given community service hours as our sentence.

But, interestingly, in the jail, we were allowed to congregate together in an open area outside the cells. One of the men I met, John, told me that he was involved in an apologetics ministry in Denver. That reminded me of Tom Trento, the guy I'd met at our men's Bible study years earlier who had helped us move. I asked John if he knew Tom and it turned out that he and Tom were part-ners in the ministry. He told me that Tom had moved to Florida, to Delray Beach. How interesting, as we were now making plans to move down to that very area! So when I got out of jail the next day, I gave Tom a call.

"Tom, this is Ira Brawer; do you remember me? I met you through Wayne up in Estes Park. You helped me move."

"Yeah, I remember you—what's up?"

"Well, I met your former partner, John, while in jail for Operation Rescue, and he mentioned that you had moved to South Florida. Since I saw you last, I have come to faith in Jesus, and Gloria and I are moving to south Florida to start a Messianic con-gregation in that area. I was wondering if we could connect and if you could help us get settled."

"Absolutely! Let me know when you are coming, and I will see what I can do to help you."

MOVING TO SOUTH FLORIDA

Shortly after, we decided that I would make another trip down there to do some scouting and see about the housing situation.

While I was visiting in the Delray Beach area, I was still thinking that we were supposed to start the congregation in West Palm Beach. Tom introduced me to the Smith family, who were neighbors of his in Delray Beach. They had a small apartment above their garage that they called the "Elisha Room," which they used to help visiting missionaries and others find temporary housing. They embraced the idea of helping us start a congregation, and were more than happy to let us stay in the Elisha room as long as we needed to.

One of the big issues in considering the move to Florida continued to be finances. When we left Estes Park in 1986, I had chalked up a huge amount of debt from the failed development projects. While in Colorado Springs, I started to get threatening letters, judgments, calls from debt collectors, and the like. At this point, there was no way I was ever going to repay this debt. So I reluctantly found a lawyer who helped us declare bankruptcy. Although I knew that, biblically, we are to pay our debts, I felt that this was part of God's grace in giving me a second chance. From that day forward, I determined to be a better steward, and even in the midst of our most difficult financial times, I made a commitment to tithe. Little by little, we learned to manage our money, putting God first with the tithe. He has been faithful ever since, and we have never gone without.

As it got closer to our time to move, I left my job at NCR and was helping Gloria in her house cleaning occupation. But, obviously, this would not provide the funds needed to make the move and start out in ministry.

We were advised to start a fundraising effort to perhaps raise the money to get started. We contacted all our believing friends and asked if they would host a "vision sharing" event for us by inviting some of their friends over for an evening. Here we would share the calling we believed God had for us to share the love of Yeshua with our Jewish people in one of the largest Jewish centers in the world, south Florida. At these gatherings, we would sing some simple Messianic songs, and I would play the guitar and share our vision, inviting them to invest in the ministry to reach the Jewish people of south Florida with the Good News that their Messiah has come. In addition to these home meetings, we also appealed to some of the Messianic leaders in the area with whom we had developed relationships through conferences in New Mexico, and through the UMJC.

As a result, we were able to raise a good amount of money upfront to help us move and get settled and cover about fifty percent of our monthly needs. We knew that we would have to work to supplement the income as well.

At the same time, I was also finishing up my degree program and the work for my ordination. We came up with a plan for Gloria to fly home to Mississippi with the girls and for me to stay behind to finish closing up our household. I then drove down and joined her at her parents' house for a few days; then we headed down to Florida. The next chapter in our lives would now begin.

We knew that God had called us to south Florida, specifically, Palm Beach County. At the time, it had the third largest population of Jewish people, after Israel and New York. We connected with the Smiths and took up residence in their Elisha room above the garage. We saw that Palm Beach was a huge county, with over one million residents, twenty percent of whom were Jewish, spread out all over the county. We were still thinking that perhaps God was calling us to West Palm Beach to plant the congregation. Although we were welcome to stay with the Smiths as long as we needed to, we knew that we had to settle where our new congregation would be and find housing for our family.

One thing I noticed pretty quickly in the area was that there were a lot of folks from New York and New Jersey, which gave the atmosphere a sense of familiarity. For Gloria, however, having grown up in a small town in Mississippi, it was a total culture shock. Generally speaking, where she came from and also in Colorado, people were usually friendly and not in a hurry. We quickly learned that south Florida was not like that at all.

CHAPTER 18
THIS IS IT

One day, shortly after we arrived in Florida, I was on an errand that took me through Boca Raton, a wealthy and expensive area in south Palm Beach County. So, driving through all the manicured yards, flowers, and expensive homes in a sub-tropical environment of palm trees and plants growing everywhere, was quite a refreshing change from dry Colorado.

As I was driving through Boca seeing all this beauty and wealth, I had this conversation with God about where He wanted us. The conversation went, something like, "Thank You, God, that you haven't called us to Boca; after all, we're not Boca people." As soon as I said that, I heard a clear response. I have only heard this type of clear voice a few times in my life, and this was definitely one of them! Loud and clear in my spirit, I heard, "This is where I want you to be!"

What! Really?" So, I go back to where we are staying and tell Gloria, "I heard the voice of the Lord. He is saying that He wants to plant us in Boca."

"What? But we are not Boca people!"

"I know; I said the same thing, but apparently God has other ideas."

From that moment on, we knew that Boca was where we were to settle and plant the work that He had called us to.

Around this time, Tom introduced me to his pastor, Jan Saatem, the assistant pastor at a large church in Boca, Spanish River Church. This relationship would prove to be very significant going forward.

Jan invited me to teach a Sunday School class on the Jewish roots of Christianity, which we decided to call "Lox and Bagels 101." It was my first teaching opportunity in this environment. A lot of people came out for it. I realized there was a hunger in many Christian hearts to know more about the Jewish background of the New Testament, the Jewishness of Jesus, Israel, and how it all fits together. As it would turn out, this would become an important part of the ministry: speaking in churches, sharing about the importance of Jewish people hearing the gospel in its Jewish context, doing Passover presentations and seders, and showing how everything that Yeshua did in His life was in line with the Torah. People needed to clearly know that He never intended to "start a new religion." It occurred to me that this teaching was following in the footsteps of my mentor and spiritual father, Eliezer, whose whole life consisted of these very things.

In the Sunday school class, there were two couples that we became close to. One was Gentile and the other was Jewish, both of whom were members of the church. January 1991 was when we had our first meeting, and we were still living in the Elisha room. The Smiths allowed us to meet in their living room, and that Friday night, several people from the church Sunday School class attended. Our meetings were very simple; we would light Shabbat candles, sing a few songs of worship; then I would teach. Shortly after, we were able to rent a house in Delray Beach and started having regular Friday night meetings.

Around the same time, we received the news that Gloria was pregnant again. We now needed a bigger vehicle than our small car. In one of our monthly newsletters to subscribers with prayer needs and praise reports, we shared this need, and someone responded by donating a van! Shortly after, we had two magnetic signs made, "Proclaiming Yeshua (Jesus), the Jewish Messiah!" Driving around with that in south Florida was interesting, and we sometimes got dirty looks and worse from Jewish people. Thankfully, most Jewish people are not violent!

CHAPTER 19
UNPLANNED BLESSINGS

Over Christmas break in 1991, Sammi and Seth came down to visit. Gloria was almost full-term with our third child, and Sammi was a senior in high school, considering colleges. One of those possibilities was the University of Florida in Gainesville; it was about a four-hour drive from Delray Beach, where we lived. One day, I took both Sammi and Seth for a drive up to Gainesville to look at the college. Sammi was a straight A student and a good candidate for UF. However, that was not to be, as we would find out a couple of months later.

In February 1992, Gloria and I welcomed our son Avi into the world. His full name is Avraham Natan: *Avraham* is the Hebrew for Abraham, and *Natan* is Nathan, meaning "gift." He truly was a gift, as were all our children. Eight days later, as is the command in the Torah, we arranged to have a *brit milah* (covenant of circumcision). We found a local *mohel*, a man who is trained to perform circumcisions. Typically, this is a religious person with medical training, who performs the rite of circumcision along with the appropriate blessings and procedures. The man we found was willing to do the circumcision, even though we were Messianic, although he would go into a different room for the blessings. We invited friends from the congregation and others, as well as my Uncle Leon and Aunt Anita.

Uncle Leon and Aunt Anita had a house in Boca, and they were basically "snow birds." This is a name for people who only come

123

to Florida in the winter from up north, New York and New Jersey. While we were still in Colorado, we let them know that we were moving to South Florida to start a Messianic congregation. At first, they were a little standoffish. However, they really connected with our kids. Since their grandchildren were up north and our kids did not have any grandparents nearby, they became their "de facto" grandparents. They would regularly take us all out to dinner, or have us over, and buy gifts for the kids at Hanukkah and birthdays. When Avi was born, we asked them to be godparents, as is customary at the brits, though usually it would be the grandparents.

Whenever I would see Uncle Leon, I would recall his words to me when I was eleven or twelve, that one day I would be a rabbi. I thought he was crazy at the time. Little did I know how prophetic those words were! Uncle Leon was a third generation butcher, and his company Lobel Meats would become well known nationally for their prime meats and enjoyed a very exclusive and wealthy clientele.

At the *bris*, I asked Uncle Leon to be the sandek, which is like the godfather. Typically that honor is given to the grandfather. How appropriate it was recalling his solemn words at my dad's funeral that, "I will be your father now", saying that with his hand on the coffin.

That night, we were glowing in the blessings of the day when I got a phone call from Sammi that would throw us for a loop. I was telling her about the bris; then asked how she was doing. She began to tell me about preparations for her senior prom, but then said that she didn't think she would be able to fit into her prom dress. I jokingly said, "Why? You're not pregnant, are you?" There is a momentary pause, and her reply would shake me to the core.

"Yes, as a matter of fact, I am!"

WHAT? She proceeded to tell me that she was actually seven months pregnant and didn't want to tell anyone for fear that her mother would make her have an abortion. The father was David, literally the "boy next door," only a couple of years older, and he had come to visit us with Sammi one weekend while we were still living in Colorado Springs. At the time, we were not impressed with him, but we accepted him because Sammi liked him. But now, what was going to happen?

I was devastated. I'm new to ministry, and my daughter is pregnant! I was terribly disappointed, but at the same time, I knew I had to support her. Then I thought, "She knew she was pregnant when they came for Christmas break and we drove up to Gainsville!" I realized that she was in denial, and she later admitted to me that she was hoping for a miscarriage. I asked her what David's situation was, and she told me that they had broken up. He already had another girlfriend and she had gotten pregnant too, but had a miscarriage.

When Gloria and I had a discussion about the situation, she wanted to call David and read him the riot act. However, I was reluctant to engage with him right now. This was one of those moments when my passivity and desire to avoid conflict (which actually had been a life pattern since my parents' divorce), would shape my behavior. Gloria was quite the opposite, and wanted to resolve, confront, and speak her mind, so I finally said, "Okay, go ahead and call him."

So she called him and confronted him regarding his plans. "What do you want to do?" she asked.

"I want to be with Sammi and be a father to this baby," he replied.

"In that case, you need to zip it up and take a lot of cold showers!" she told him, in typical Gloria style.

I immediately made plans to go visit Sammi to help her decide what to do. I already knew that Sammi and her mom did not have a good relationship, and as her dad, I had to be there for her. So I went to Colorado and spent some time with both Sammi and David separately. I was thinking that the best solution at this time was for Sammi to give the baby up for adoption. She was going to graduate at the top of her class and had her college career to look forward to. Humanly, that seems like the best solution. But it clearly wasn't God's solution. She was determined to keep the baby and be a mom. I also met with David to see what his intentions were. He clearly said that he wanted to be a dad and be with Sammi. So I advised him to get his act together. He seemed sincere, but we would see.

Because of her high grades, Sammi was given the favor of not having to come back to school until graduation in June. Jordan was born on April 30. So now we have a son and a grandson that are ten weeks apart. Imagine little Avi as an uncle at ten weeks old!

We returned to Colorado in June for Sammi's graduation, joined by my mom. She had moved to Las Vegas and came to see her first great-grandchild. We had a big pow wow, with David, Sammi, his parents, and my mom. In that meeting, it was decided that Sammi would come down to Florida with Jordan to get away for a while, maybe for the summer. At that time we had a fairly small three bedroom house in Delray Beach, but of course we welcomed the opportunity for Sammi to be with us.

So Sammi and Jordan flew down to visit us around the first week of the following month, July 1992. When we asked about her return flight, her reply was that she didn't have one. Slowly, we started to realize that she was intending to stay, and not go back to Colorado. That was definitely a wonderful surprise for us, and somehow, we knew that with God's help we could make it work. At this time, we were still only a year or so into the new ministry, and money was very tight. The congregation was not yet sufficiently established to pay us a salary, so we depended on the monthly support that we raised. Often, there were unexpected donations that we would find in the mailbox—usually when needed the most. Gloria was still cleaning houses, and I had a part-time job delivering newspapers. We trusted in God for His provision, and He never let us down.

So now we had Josie, who was seven; Micha who was three; Avi and Jordan, both pretty much infants; and Sammi. We moved Avi into our room, the girls shared a room, and Sammi and Jordan had the third bedroom. Sammi enrolled in the community college, and while she was at school, Gloria took care of the boys. It was like having twins except that Avi was always much bigger than Jordan; but they were adorable together. I pretty much worked from home and was able to pitch in when Gloria was out at work. Sammi also started to attend the congregation with us.

David stayed in touch with Sammi. He insisted that he wanted to be together with her and be a dad to Jordan. But meanwhile, he had gotten into trouble with the law and was on probation. About six months after Sammi and Jordan came to live with us, David decided to come down to Florida and pursue the relationship. We were able to get him a room to stay in with a couple of single men we knew who were believers in Yeshua. We laid down some pretty strict rules for them as they spent time together.

Sammi and Jordan were still living with us, and when she was out with David, we were watching Jordan. There were some tense moments where we wondered if this was going to work. We also insisted that they all come to the congregation regularly as well. David had no knowledge of the faith, either from a Jewish or traditional Christian perspective. He had no religious upbringing, but he seemed open. Then, on Yom Kippur, 1993, David accepted Yeshua as his Savior. Ironically, it was on the same night that I had my Yeshua experience nine years before. Things began to improve after that, and they seemed ready to get married, which is what we were all praying and hoping for. I referred them to my friend, Pastor Jan Sattem, and he took them through premarital counseling. In December of that year, I had the privilege of marrying them.

Over the next four years, they had two more boys, Joshua and Joseph. In 1997, they decided to move back to Colorado, and there they had number four, a girl named Kaylee. I often look back on this event and others and reflect on how good God is. Even in our bad choices, He is merciful and kind, and what our adversary intended to harm us, God can turn around and use both for our good and His glory. This is one of those times when the word of God spoken through the prophet Jeremiah rings so true:

"For I know the plans I have in mind for you, plans for well-being, not for bad things, so that you can have hope and a future" (Jeremiah 29:11, Complete Jewish Bible).

While these words were spoken to Israel to comfort them in the midst of the calamity of exile, they are equally reassuring to us in all our challenges. It certainly has been true for me. It took me a long time to understand that God is truly on my side, that He does have my best interests at heart, and that He does have "hope and a future" for me, my children, and grandchildren. He is for us, merciful and kind.

As we continued to meet on Friday night, and I continued to teach at the church, we saw God's hand, blessing what we were doing. After about six months of meeting in our little house, we needed to find a bigger space to meet, so we started meeting at a local high school, still on Friday nights. Our goal was to move to Saturday mornings to have a regular Shabbat morning service.

Over the next year or so, as more people joined us, we decided to make the change. It was becoming clear that we had the makings of a congregation, and we began the process of formalizing ourselves. We met an attorney who offered to help us pro bono. She incorporated the congregation under the name Ayts Chayim Messianic Synagogue (Tree of Life). We were surprised to know that some of the people who were joining us on Friday nights were not going to stay with us as we moved to Saturday morning. Some of them were attending another church on Sunday mornings as well, but as we became more formal in our development, they were no longer able to continue. We were fine with that. We viewed those people as the "scaffolding," necessary in the early stages of a building, but not necessary once the building is constructed. I mean, we were far from a finished building, but we understood the concept and were fine with it.

However, the first two couples in the group stayed with us, and together they became the original board members as we chartered the congregation. At the ceremonial banquet, our guest speaker was Marty Waldman, the friend I made a few years earlier at the conference in Glorietta, NM, the very one who had counseled us to plant a new congregation rather than join a missions organization. By now, we had about fifteen charter members in our small congregation, mostly Jewish, but also some Gentiles.

Early on, we understood that, while the vision God had given us was to reach our Jewish people with the love of Yeshua, He would also bring in faithful Gentiles with a heart for Israel and the Jewish people to come alongside us.

Some of those foundational members stayed with us for many years. One of those couples was Seymour and Lita Kurtzer, a very typical older Jewish couple from New York. The house we rented in Delray Beach turned out to be down the street from them, and they became good friends and surrogate grandparents to our children. Then there was Frieda Rothberg, also a typical older Jewish widow from New York. The difference was that they were believers in Yeshua, and had caught the vision to join us in the planting of Ayts Chayim. They became integral parts of our growing little community, and were with us until the end of their lives on earth, twenty-five or so years later.

CHAPTER 20
ENTER THE HOLY SPIRIT

While still in Colorado Springs, we met Alyosha and Jody, a Messianic Jewish couple who lived in Maryland. Alyosha, a gifted classical piano player in the Ukraine, had escaped with his family in the 1970s and become a follower of Yeshua. Jody was a Jewish-American woman who also came to faith in Yeshua. Alyosha composed classical style worship music that was wonderful. They had come to our congregation in Colorado Springs and ministered in music as well as shared. They subsequently moved to Ormond Beach, Florida, which is near Daytona Beach, and were part of a Messianic congregation there.

One day, we got a call from them saying they would like to come down and visit. It seemed important. We were happy to receive them, although at the time we had only met them once. They needed some counsel and support as they were having a disagreement with their leader. At this time, I was the regional director of the UMJC, the organization that we had first connected with in Colorado Springs. There had been a bitter feud between the two main Messianic Jewish organizations, the UMJC and the MJAA (Messianic Jewish Alliance of America). You might be wondering, *Is the Messianic movement that big to have two organizations?* It speaks to the old adage, "Where you have two Jews, you have three opinions!"

So as the regional director, part of my job was to recruit new congregations into the UMJC. This did not endear me to the Alliance congregations in the southeast, which were far more in number. I was helping groups to form that had come out of some of these congregations, and encouraging them to connect to the UMJC. So when Alyosha and Jody came to see us, it was partly to get some encouragement from friends and partly to get some advice from me as regional director about starting another congregation. During the time that we met, they were telling us about a revival that was going on in a church in central Florida.

My theological view at this stage of my life and ministry was that the moment a person came to faith in Yeshua, he received all of the Holy Spirit. All this other stuff about speaking in tongues, falling down, laughter, and so on was just the latest hype and not of God—just more charisma. So, we had a good laugh over this (in a mocking way), and they spent a couple of days with us. We became closer friends as we still are to this day.

Some months later, we scheduled a special Shabbat service where we invited Dr. Louis Goldberg to come and speak. Alyosha was invited to come and play the piano. This was in January 1994. When they got to us, I immediately noticed that there was something different about Alyosha. Previously quite reserved and introverted, he was extremely vocal about what he had experienced that week. He and Jody had gone to some of the meetings of the same preacher that we were mocking a few months earlier, and now they had an encounter with God that "changed him."

He started telling me about how great his times at the revival meetings were and that we needed to go up there as well. I was really annoyed because my focus was on the special Shabbat service we were having the next day, and I had no interest in driving three hours to Lakeland to hear this guy and get into his message about the Holy Spirit or anything else. But Alyosha kept on talking about it. Gloria came home, and he was still going on about how God "touched him" and that we should go. I was still not interested.

"What if there was a million dollars waiting for you there? Would you go?" was his final appeal.

I finally had to say, "Yes."

His response to me was, "This is better than a million dollars."

However, we were reluctant and were beginning to consider some convenient excuses. One, we didn't have the money to go up to Lakeland and stay at a hotel. Two, Josie was in school, and we couldn't pull her out to take her with us. And three, Josie was not feeling well. "So there," I said, "There's no way we could go."

Still not daunted, Alyosha challenged us, "Would you pray about it and see if God wants you to go?"

I agreed to do that because I was pretty sure those were solid excuses. Well, we went ahead with our special Shabbat morning service, not thinking too much about this possible trip to Lakeland, when, lo and behold, all three of my excuses vanished. First, we were given an anonymous gift of $300 personally. This was quite unusual because as a congregation, people generally give their tithes and offerings to the congregation. It was unusual that there would be a special gift designated for us. Second, Gloria spoke to one of Josie's friend's mom, and she was more than happy to have Josie stay with her for a couple of days. And three, Josie made a "miraculous recovery" from being sick.

Now I was out of excuses and had to admit that perhaps God actually wanted us to go. So we arranged to pack up Micha, who was five at this time, and Avi, who was almost two years old, and make the trip up to Central Florida, where the "camp meetings" were being held, but without the camp and in a church. There were morning and night meetings for a week.

The first meeting we attended was on a Monday morning. The service started out with very lively worship music. We were not used to this kind of worship music, as much as Messianic Jewish type songs, which have their own style. This was very "Gentile," but yet it was worshipful. After the worship music, there was an invitation for anyone who needed physical healing to come up. Gloria still had a bad knee from the car accident we had years ago in Colorado, so she went forward in hopes that her knee would be healed. She stood in line with others and was prayed for. She came back to where we were sitting, and the first thing I asked was, "How's your knee?"

"I don't know about my knee, but something better happened, I felt God's presence, and it was like a blanket of peace," she answered.

The next thing was an invitation to pray for those who were ministering to the nations. Our friend, Jody, was at that morning meeting, and she encouraged me, "Ira, you are a minister to Israel; you should go up."

So, I did, and for the first time in the nearly ten years that I had been a follower of Yeshua, I experienced in that moment the tangible presence of God. I felt engulfed by God's love and peace. I had never felt anything like that before. I came back to where we were sitting, and Gloria immediately asked me, "So what happened?"

I was at a loss for words other than, "I felt the presence of the Holy Spirit." But my current theology was being shaken. I was at another one of those pivotal moments that would affect me, our family, our congregation, and many others in the years ahead.

After a couple of days of morning and evening services, we came home. Over the next year, I would spend many hours reading and studying about the Holy Spirit. I read several books that described historical revivals and present-day outpourings that have been going on. I re-read various Scripture verses regarding the Holy Spirit, particularly in the Book of Acts, which is really a history of the earliest followers of Yeshua from His resurrection to the next thirty years.

In re-reading the stories and encounters of these earliest followers of Yeshua, I looked at the interactions and manifestations of the Holy Spirit in a way that I had not seen before. Having now had a personal experience—even for a moment—I had greater insight into the outworking and empowerment of the Holy Spirit for believers to live radical lives as Yeshua's disciples. I also began to teach on Shabbat about the Holy Spirit and His importance in our lives to guide us as our Helper as Yeshua describes (John 14), but also His supernatural outworking for healings and demonstration of miracles.

This understanding also began to change my prayer life and my relationship with God. I began to understand more about His love and mercy, and that He truly is a good Father. I also began to see how I had put God in a box in my limited understanding of Him. But I had a long way to go, and there would be more revelation and understanding about the working of God and His Spirit. There would also be major conflict within our fledgling congregation.

As January 1995 came around, we planned to spend a whole week at the revival's winter camp meeting. The kids came along with us as they also had a children's program. We were determined to go to each meeting, morning and evening, to receive all that God had for us. If you just walked into one of these services, it would seem like there was chaos and disorder. People were laughing, crying, and literally falling down in the Spirit. As we started out with the first meetings, we began to understand what was happening, and at the same time, we weren't necessarily entering into the same experiences. However, we stayed open, enjoying the worship and the teaching. I was learning a lot of principles regarding the Holy Spirit and, at the same time, allowing Him to do whatever was needed in my heart.

One evening I had a dramatic experience, not outwardly, but in my heart. It had to do with this revelation of God as my *Abba*, which is a Hebrew word similar to "Daddy." God showed me that He wasn't like my earthly dad. While my dad was a good man, he was emotionally detached from me growing up, and mostly into his own work and, after the divorce, his social life. Also growing in Judaism, God is not seen as a personal God, but as distant and punishing.

There was a moment that evening where there was an altar call, and I went up. I had an emotional experience where I believe that God revealed His heart as my Abba to me. I knew in my head that I had that personal relationship with God because of what Yeshua did; He made the way to the Father (John 14:6). But it is one thing to understand it intellectually, and another when He makes His presence known dramatically. It was really the beginning of a much more intimate relationship with Him.

More and more, I was beginning to understand how my relationship with God is really a journey. It's a journey similar to marriage, where there are bumps along the way. But as you continue on that journey, along with the challenges, you begin to get to know the other person more and more. You also realize that this relationship is not about you; it is about the other person. In this case, it is growing in intimacy with the One who knows me better than anyone else.

Continuing in that week, we came to Friday, the last day of the camp meeting. At the morning service when Gloria and I came in, we decided to sit separately because all week we would keep turning to each other during the service and asking, "Are you feeling anything? Are you getting anything?" Maybe by not being next to each other, we could more freely "enter in" and experience what God had for us more fully.

So I sat in a row next to a few men that I didn't know. The worship was going on, and we were all standing. All of a sudden, the guy next to me falls back in the pew. I look over and think, "Wow, that's strange!" The next moment, I felt something hit me, and I too was knocked back to the pew. The next moment, I felt this thing coming up from my stomach and out of my mouth—loud and uncontrollable laughter! I was laughing so hard that I fell out of the pew altogether and found myself lying on the floor in the aisle. Still laughing uncontrollably, I began to feel a tingling, like an electric current running through my hands and my mouth. At that moment, I felt like I heard God say, "I am anointing your mouth for preaching and your hands for praying."

I was laid out for about an hour and couldn't move. Getting up, I experienced for the first time being "drunk in the spirit," reminding me of the disciples in Acts 2, where Peter says that "these men are not drunk as you suppose." Apparently, they were filled with the Holy Spirit and acting like drunk people. I knew at that moment that my life was about to change. I didn't realize though exactly how much or what.

When Gloria and I reconnected, I shared my experience with her. We were both super excited about the experiences this week, and we decided to stay for the evening service. It was amazing. I had never felt so free in my life. I knew at that moment that my life and my relationship with God, and the ministry of the congregation would never be the same!

We drove home that evening and were excited to get to the congregation the next morning. We arrived home at around 3:00 a.m. and got a couple of hours of sleep. I did not have a prepared message for the morning service, which is already unusual for me. I decided to take the opportunity to use the Torah portion of the week from Exodus about the Israelites being freed to talk about true freedom, and I shared my own experience of the week at the revival meetings.

When we came into the service, I was still feeling very high in the Spirit. I guess I had a big grin on my face. It must have shown, because a couple of people asked Gloria, "What's up with the Rabbi? He looks different." Little did they know how different!

The service starts, and the time for my message comes. I start by summarizing the Torah portion about the freeing of the slaves from Egyptian bondage. I begin to share about spiritual freedom. During that time, Lita, an older Jewish lady in our congregation, gets up quite spontaneously and brings me a glass of water. (Later she would say she just felt prompted by the Spirit to get up and get me that water.) I begin to share something like, "So last year when we went to the camp meetings, I got a little taste of what it is …" and I took a little sip of the water "… like this." "This year," I continued, "it was more like this," and then I poured the glass of water on my head! Well, that got the people's attention!

I ended the message, and for the first time, I invited anyone who wanted to receive what I had to come up. Lita was the first one, and others also followed. As I touched her head and prayed for her, she fell back to the floor. Others I prayed for had similar experiences. People began to laugh and experience similar things that I had experienced previously at the camp meetings. So it began. As God began to move and set people free, the atmosphere in the congregation changed dramatically. In my naiveté, I assumed that everyone would embrace this "move of the Spirit." Boy, was I wrong!

In this period of time, we averaged around seventy to eighty people on a typical Shabbat service. We ended up losing about half that number. This was hard, but I knew that what we had experienced was real, and, while it was sad to lose these people, I felt like the blind man that was healed by Yeshua. When interrogated by the religious leaders, all he could say was, "I was blind, and now I see." I could not go back to the way it was. I was determined to set a new course where the Holy Spirit was now welcome in all our services. The ones that stayed were hungry to see and experience this move of God in their lives.

This season of free-flowing services lasted for hours, praying for people, seeing them receive healing, and deepening their relationship with God. It went on for a couple of years. During that time, we also had other special speakers and ministers who were also operating in the same flow of the Holy Spirit. Over time, however, we realized that people had stopped growing; they were more interested in the "high" of the experience, rather than using the experience to go deeper in their relationship with God. There were other spiritual dynamics at work, and we began to realize more and more that we were in a spiritual battle. The enemy of our souls was certainly out to destroy our congregation through division, offenses, gossip, and false accusation. As a result, the congregation dwindled in number over this period.

CHAPTER 21
DISRUPTION AND CHANGE

There was a Jewish man, David, who was a friend of one of our members who I had led to Yeshua and mentored. David became my right-hand man. Shortly after, a Jewish woman, Bobbi, came into the congregation who was experienced in ministry. Eventually they wanted to get married, and I married them. Before long, an issue arose between us and rather than work it out, they chose to leave and start their own congregation.

Another time a Jewish man named Russ that had come to faith in the congregation became a right-hand man to me. His wife had been offended over something, and they also left. But with David and Bobbi it was more hurtful because of the level of trust and responsibility that was accorded them. Betrayal is a curious thing because it's easy to feel like you are the victim. *How could they do that to me?* David and Bobbi left after a disagreement and they decided that they were going to start their own congregation.

This was the start of several betrayals that I was to experience. I later realized how in many cases my woundedness from the past, mainly over my parents' divorce, would impact me and contribute to my part in these betrayals. I realized it was about my need to be needed, my passive-aggressive tendencies, and the devastation I experienced when there was disagreement.

Some of these patterns would follow us in the years to come until the time came when we knew we needed to get some healing from our own past wounds. We began to understand how those past hurts and wounds were still affecting our relationships with others, and even our marriage relationship. Yes, unhealed wounds from the past were literally open doors to experiencing the same type of hurt, over and over again. There was a moment we wondered how we could even continue in the ministry with so much betrayal all around. So, between people leaving because of the issue of the Holy Spirit and this issue with David and Bobbi, our congregation shrank to about twenty-five people.

In one of those moments, I remember very clearly complaining to God. His response was "What if I only gave you these twenty-five? Would you pour your life into them?"

There was only one answer, "Yes, Lord, please forgive me for complaining and being discontent. I will be happy to pour my life into these that You have given me." I was deeply convicted, and that moment changed everything for me. My attitude became more about the people than about me and my ego.

One day I was working in the yard, pruning some of the trees, and there was this little scrawny one that I thought of just pulling out. But, after I pruned back some of the dead branches, I could see that it had good potential. As I looked at it, I heard God's voice say, "Just as you are pruning the tree, so am I pruning Ayts Chayim (remember Tree of Life is the name of our congregation at this time). Things changed after that, and He began to bring in new people.

About twenty-five years later, after only seeing us a couple of times at conferences, David and Bobbi called and wanted to get together with Gloria and me. We met in a deli. Bobbi was suffering from cancer and was in a wheelchair. While we were sitting there eating breakfast, they both repented and asked for forgiveness for the way they had left the congregation so many years earlier. We, of course, forgave them. Sadly, Bobbi passed away a few months later.

Around this time, I ran into Dan Juster at a conference. I was having trouble navigating the balance of having this revival type move of the Holy Spirit in the congregation while maintaining the Messianic vision. The experiences that we had at the camp meetings were in a Pentecostal culture. The challenge that I now had was how to fulfill the vision that God called us to as a Messianic Jewish congregation with the emphasis on reaching Jewish people with the love of Yeshua. At the same time, we could not deny the experiences and the deeper understanding of the work of the Holy Spirit. Were those two concepts contradictory? Was there a way to blend them? I knew that Dan, besides being one of the top theologians in our movement, was also the leader of a successful Messianic congregation in Maryland that had experienced the move of the Holy Spirit. Perhaps by talking to him I could gain some insight into these questions.

His wise counsel boiled down to the idea that we must separate the reality of the Holy Spirit working, from the cultural context in which He moves. We had inadvertently adopted in our service some of the music and style that we saw at the camp meetings. However, as a Messianic congregation reaching out to the Jewish community, we still needed to maintain our distinctly Messianic Jewish expression of worship, including some of the important traditions like the Torah service and some of the traditional prayers. This is what makes us unique, and what Jewish people who come to visit can identify with.

The other aspect of ministry that Dan spoke to me about was establishing a more formal leadership structure. At present, I was the only elder in the congregation, while our by-laws stated that the government of the congregation was to be a board of elders based on the model and teaching of the New Covenant communities. But up until now there were no other men mature enough to qualify to join me at that level of leadership. Dan was starting to form an association of several congregations that he either helped start or was in close relationship with. This association, or network, is called *Tikkun*. Tikkun is a Hebrew word meaning "to repair" or "to restore" from the term *Tikkun Olam*, meaning "repairing the world," a common Jewish concept of serving. As Dan explained the vision for Tikkun, I become more and more interested. What he was sharing seemed to be a fit for us.

The basic vision of the network is a close association among the member congregations that have a Messianic vision along with openness to the Holy Spirit and the gifts of the Spirit as described in the New Covenant Scriptures. The network had an annual conference where the worship was free-flowing, and included the gifts of the Spirit such as prophetic words and praying for individuals. After careful discussion, we made a decision to join the Network which became a spiritual covering or authority for us.

The importance of spiritual covering is a concept that I was just beginning to understand. The basic idea is that God has established various spheres of authority and structure for our protection and provision, in the home, the workplace, the government, and the local congregation. In these spheres of authority that are set up for our good, God wants us to respect and submit to these authorities with a couple of exceptions. The main exception is when the authority requires us to do something that contradicts God's Word; in such a case, we are to put God's Word above the authority, such as during times of religious persecution by the government itself. The other time is when there is a violation of our conscience or a strong conviction that we are also to resist the authority, although we must realize we must be prepared for any social consequences.

We joined the Tikkun network, and it became a spiritual covering for us. In this process I begin to understand that associated with this idea of authority is the concept of one needing to be *under* authority if you are to be *in* authority. When Yeshua was approached by a Roman centurion asking Him to heal his servant, Yeshua agreed to go to this man's house, which in itself was highly unusual because, according to His own words, "I came only to the lost sheep of the house of Israel." In other words, He did not come primarily for the Gentiles at this stage. However, this centurion appealed on the basis of faith, and that he was also a believer in the God of Israel, which was unusual for a Roman soldier. He demonstrated even more faith when he told Yeshua that it was not necessary for Him to enter his house, as he too was "a man under authority, and I tell this one to go and he goes, and that one to come and he comes" (Matthew 8:8). The principle here is that the Roman, as a middle level officer, had superiors he had to submit to and soldiers and servants under him that he directed. The principle that we learn from this story is that in order to have genuine spiritual authority, we must be willing to submit to higher authority. In a sense, I had been unconsciously operating in this principle for quite some time. Even before Yom Kippur moment when I opened my heart to Yeshua, I had always looked to teachers to help guide me on my journey.

Now, becoming part of the Tikkun network conformed to that pattern. The values we upheld of a strong faith in Yeshua, Jewish expression, operating in the gifts and the power of the Holy Spirit, and a healthy authority structure, became the foundational principles that now drove me forward as in building the congregation in Boca.

The vision of our congregation of thirty-two years has been the same:

"We are a congregation of Jewish followers of Yeshua and believing Gentiles who worship together. We serve God's calling for the return of the Jewish people to a relationship with the God of our fathers through faith in Yeshua the Messiah."

I have long had this deep conviction in my heart. Just as I, a Jewish boy raised in a traditional Jewish home with the traditional aversion to anything Christian and especially toward Jesus Himself, have finally surrendered to Him. And now as a Rabbi establishing and leading a Messianic congregation, would with His help create a safe environment where Jewish people could come and explore the possibility that He is the One we have been waiting for. What He has done for me, He would do for anyone who desires, not just head knowledge based on evidence, but the transformation that comes with surrender in our hearts to Him.

As the congregation grew, we saw different people, Jews and Gentiles, coming in from different backgrounds. While our emphasis was on attracting Jewish people we also recognized that there would always be Gentiles who felt called to worship and to learn in the context of Messianic congregations. We knew early on that the folks that would be most attracted to the congregation would be those of "interfaith" marriages, that is, a Jewish person married to a Gentile, such as the case with Gloria and me. Also, our heart is for families, and so as we had our three children, we attracted other families with small children as well. We established a Shabbat school, with classes for children on Shabbat morning prior to the service, recognizing the importance of training our children with a biblical foundation. We also established adult Shabbat classes for teaching the adults about how to grow in faith and community. It always is amazing to see the people that God has brought to us, the families from all the different backgrounds and upbringings.

CHAPTER 22
NEW OPPORTUNITIES

One Shabbat morning in 1995, we had a visitor to the congregation from Nicaragua. He was a pastor of a church in the capital, Managua. He was in the country attending a conference, when he met someone familiar with our congregation, who suggested he come and meet us. Pastor Daniel Ortega had a deep love for Israel, and his church prayed regularly for Israel. We met after the service, and Pastor Daniel invited Gloria and me to come to his church to speak. I really did not take the invitation too seriously, as I knew that there had recently been a civil war there and it was probably the last place on earth that I would think about visiting.

So I said, "Sure, maybe we will come," trying to be polite but knowing that I had no intention of actually going to Nicaragua. But God had other ideas, as He often does. A couple of weeks after, we get an envelope in the mail with two airline tickets to Managua! This was serious! These were poor people, and for him to buy us tickets and send them to us showed he meant business. And so did God! So we made plans to go. This was in December of that year, before Christmas and what an amazing trip it turned out to be!

As I mentioned, the country had just gone through a civil war. We learned that Nicaragua, while a beautiful country, was the poorest country in all of Central America. However, we found the people in this church, though mostly poor, were generous in heart. They welcomed us with open arms. The first night we arrived we saw a live volcano up close, with lava pouring out. Nicaragua is situated geographically in a volcanic region and experiences eruptions from time to time. There was a major earthquake in the 1970s that destroyed much of the capital city of Managua. The infrastructure of the country was a mess—roads had big potholes, and traffic was crazy with no lanes on the roads. That first night we didn't get back to our hotel room until about 6:00 a.m., and we were covered with soot from the volcano. We only had a couple of hours when we would be picked up to go to the church for the first of several special meetings for me to teach and speak about Israel, and our lives as Messianic Jews. The people were warm and receptive. We came to realize that those who have little materially are often more excited and on fire about their relationship with God than those of us who live in relative comfort. It was an incredibly life-changing and encouraging experience. We were taken around to see the surroundings and spoke at a few other churches.

For the next ten years, we would go to Nicaragua every year for around ten days. On various trips we took our youth group, our own kids, and adults who were missions-minded. In every case, the experience had a lasting effect on all who attended. On the various trips we went into a prison, a leper colony, brought food and helped with humanitarian projects and we started bringing crates of clothing with us on each trip. We developed some strong relationships with the people in the church, and one couple even had a baby named after me!

Wherever we went, Pastor Daniel encouraged me to speak about Israel and God's eternal plan and purpose for the Jewish people. This blessed the people immensely. On one trip we brought a friend of ours, Paul Wilbur, a well-known Messianic worship leader. We had a concert that brought many people from the city. Paul worked with their worship team and they translated some of his songs into Spanish. As a result of that trip, Paul went on to produce much of his music in Spanish and visit many other Latin American countries.

Our last trip, unfortunately, did not end too well. We had a disagreement with Daniel over a financial issue, and there were accusations that were very hurtful. Sadly, we had no choice but to end the relationship. But we do look back on those trips fondly. We recognized that, while the people we ministered to were blessed to hear about Israel and to meet us, we also gained so much in that experience especially being put in inconvenient situations, such as hotels without hot water, pollution in the air from all the exhaust of old cars, lack of punctuality and planning, and other discomforts unlike our cushy environment back home. By far, the most satisfying part of our time in Nicaragua was seeing the love and appreciation of the people toward us and spending time and sharing life with them while imparting God's love.

BEIT MORESHET

As we progressed in the work of the congregation, we always had the burden of teaching and training our children. We made a decision to home school our own children, where the emphasis was on developing their character. There were other families that were drawn to the congregation that shared our values in this area. Together we established what we call "Shabbat School." This was an organized program to teach the children of the congregation about the Torah and Hebrew. They also put on plays for special holidays like Hanukkah and Purim. In this, we were applying Deuteronomy 6:5 seriously, that we are to teach our children, "When you rise up, when you lie down, and when you walk by the way."

Along with this I began to have a burden for youth and young adults in the greater Messianic movement. With that in mind I was meeting with two mentors of mine that were leaders in the

Network, Gary Kivelowitz and Carl Kinbar. In sharing the concern about raising up the next generation, we birthed a vision called *Beit Moreshet*, which is Hebrew for "Heritage House." In this process we developed strategies for reaching out to the young people.

One of the main strategies was to invite Messianic young people from all over the country for a ten-day intensive program during the summer that our congregation would host. We were able to get the word out to the various congregations, and for the next five years we held these ten-day intensives. We also visited congregations with teams of young adults for weekend youth events. Our main goal in each of these events was to impart a vision for intimacy with God, the importance of relationships, and the importance of serving in their local congregations.

In these intensives, senior leaders and teachers from within the Messianic movement would come in to impart vision to develop these young people. We would challenge them by taking them to the mall and have them speak to people about Yeshua. We also did some fun things while they were with us. Members of the congregation would host the young people in their homes. While there were challenges in putting these events together, for me the blessing was in the relationships with these young people that were developed that in some cases we still maintain even today.

Sometimes we run into some of these young people, now married with kids, and they talk about how their time in Beit Moreshet shaped their lives. We had two marriages that developed out of that pivotal time. One of the couples had just started dating when they joined us. The girl, Brooke, was from Texas, and the boy, Toby, was from Georgia. We sat down with them at the beginning of the program and asked them to refrain from "coupling up" during their time. They were totally compliant, went through the program and a few months later were engaged to be married. Now fifteen years later, they have kids, are in full time ministry, and whenever I see them they always talk about their time with us in Beit Moreshet and how it has given them a foundation for their lives.

Another couple, Aaron from San Diego, and Heather from Ohio, who were both rabbis' kids, met in our program. Not too long after they pursued a relationship and eventually got married. We were blessed to be at the wedding. They are doing great, with children and serving in their congregation in North Carolina. We also had interns whom I personally mentored that came for six months at a time, served in the congregation, and have gone on to serve and have families of their own. Just as I have placed a high value in the men that have mentored me over many years, so have I had great joy and satisfaction in helping these young people grow and mature into responsible adults. I am so proud of all three of our children for going through the ten-day intensive as well at different years.

CHAPTER 23
JOSIE MAKES ALIYAH

While home schooling our own children, we always tried to impart important spiritual principles to them. This included the importance of Israel, not only from the historical and biblical perspective, but also as a modern-day nation facing enemies all around. They also knew that we had family there, my mom's cousins.

When Josie got close to graduating high school, she began to talk about wanting to go to Israel to make *Aliyah*. Aliyah is a Hebrew word meaning "to go up." It is a term that applies to Jewish people all over the world who move to Israel under the Law of Return. When the modern nation of Israel was established in 1948, right after the horror of the Holocaust, it was to be a home for the Jewish people. It was established that a Jewish person would be eligible to become a citizen if they had at least one Jewish grandparent. According to Jewish law, a person is only Jewish if their mother is Jewish. Today, that is changing in some of the streams of Judaism to allow for patrilineal descent. That is why, in Josie's case, even with her mom not being Jewish, she was still able to make Aliyah based on my Jewishness.

This was in 2002, before the internet and Google. The reason that matters is that presently, even if you are Jewish according to the Law of Return, if it comes up that you are a follower of Yeshua, it has been determined that you have changed religions and no longer qualify for citizenship in Israel. Fortunately, many

Messianic Jewish believers did make Aliyah back before it was an issue.

Josie and Gloria went down to the Israeli consulate in Miami one day and she presented her (my) papers to establish that she qualifies to make Aliyah, although she is not considered Jewish according to rabbinic law. She received her paperwork to move forward with her Aliyah application. A few months later, she left for Israel and, as part of her program was placed in a *kibbutz* (or Israeli collective settlement) in the north part of the country.

As believers in Yeshua and having been homeschooled, our children were sheltered in many ways. Josie was full of excitement and idealism moving to Israel. She encountered other young people her age on the kibbutz from other countries, and many of them immediately start "hooking up." She right away felt like an outsider, as she would not participate. However, in a short time she was able to get settled and into the flow of working on the kibbutz and taking *Ulpan*, or intensive Hebrew classes.

We also had friends living in Israel at the time that she was able to connect with. My second cousins, Menachem and Yossi, the ones that I got to know the summer I spent in Israel with my mom, were also there for her to visit.

Shortly after Josie made Aliyah, we brought our first tour to Israel with a group of people, mostly from the congregation. We would eventually take several more tours, and in each case, we would always stay longer and visit friends and family. It was always a blessing to visit the Land—especially with Josie living there.

One day we got a call from her that she had enlisted in the army! We knew that was something she had wanted to do, but she had only been in the Land for six months and she had just turned eighteen. We thought she would wait a while before taking that step. In Israel, every boy and girl is enlisted in the Israeli army when they reach eighteen. The only exceptions are those who are on their own without family, like Josie. She was not compelled to go into the army; however, she felt very strongly that if she was going to make a life for herself in Israel, she needed to have the shared experience of all Israelis.

An Israeli soldier like Josie who is in Israel without immediate family is called a lone soldier. This has some special benefits. Also, there were benefits for doing army service, such as university tuition which was something that she wanted to do. While her Hebrew was not great, she pushed through the basic training and then signed up for a unit that was on a training base in the Negev desert. Her job? A Humvee driver on training exercises. As a typical American teenager, she had received her driver's license at sixteen. In Israel, most of the kids did not get their licenses until after their army stint. So she was a perfect fit for this position, and she loved it.

In her unit there were a lot of Russian girls whose families had immigrated after the iron curtain fell. In fact during the 1990s it was estimated that over one million Jews from the former Soviet Union made Aliyah to Israel. Now the children of these immigrants were of age for the army, and they resented Josie because they had to serve but she chose to volunteer. At first they were not very nice to her, but over time she earned their respect and they eventually voted her top soldier in the unit. On top of that, she received the Hannah Senesh award for outstanding soldier. Hannah Sennesh was a Hungarian Jew that immigrated to Palestine in 1939, then joined an elite paratrooper force and was dropped into Yugoslavia in 1941 to aid anti-Nazi forces. She was captured by the Nazis and executed. She is a hero in modern Jewish history. There was a ceremony at the Kotel (western wall) and Hannah Senesh's family was there to present the award to Josie. Unfortunately, we were not able to be there for that special event.

However, I had the opportunity to see her while on a trip with one of the families in the congregation who wanted to have their son's Bar Mitzvah in Jerusalem at the Kotel. Jewish people from around the world go to Jerusalem to have their sons' Bar Mitzvahs. In the open space by the Kotel on Mondays and Thursdays, which are Bar Mitzvah days, they set up tables all around, and you will see an incredible diversity in dress, and in the way their ceremonies are conducted depending on the culture from which they come.

It is important to understand that Jewish people over the centuries, mainly due to persecution, were dispersed to the four corners of the planet. As such, wherever our people landed, we typically adopted the culture of the countries, including the food, the music, the clothing, the language, and more. Jews in Europe, like my parents and grandparents, adopted a European culture, which was way different than Jews living in Arab lands. As a result, on any given Monday or Thursday morning at the Kotel, this diversity would be evident with twenty Bar Mitzvahs going on at the same time. Seeing the different cultures displayed at one time was quite a spectacle!

That June day in Jerusalem was a record heat. We were there "under the radar," so to speak, because if the rabbis who run this whole system found out that we were Messianic, we would be thrown out so fast we wouldn't know what hit us! We started around 9:00 a.m. with a traditional prayer; then the main part is when the Bar Mitzvah boy would read his part of the Torah. The son of the family I was performing the Bar Mitzvah ceremony for, Justin, was a small skinny kid. By that time it was so hot, Justin nearly passed out. We got through it and were packing up, next to us was a group that was obviously very orthodox, but American. They start talking to us, asking us where we are from.

"We're from Florida," we said.

"Wow, so are we; where in Florida?"

"Boca Raton," we answered as we quickly began to pack up everything, not wanting to give too much information for fear of being exposed.

"Oh, we're from Coral Springs (a neighboring town). What synagogue are you with?"

Oops, now what? "It's Ayts Chayim—but we have to get going!" and with that we hastily left.

Of course I visited Josie on her army base in the Negev. I could not have been prouder of her than to see her in her army uniform on a base with tanks and combat vehicles all around. That was definitely a highlight of that trip. After Josie finished her army duty, her desire was to go on to university, which would be paid for by the State by virtue of her completion of her army commitment. We happened to be there on another trip and went with her to the admissions office. We were terribly disappointed to find out that they would not accept her homeschool high school certificate as evidence of a high school degree. In addition, she had never taken the SAT because of her intention to move to Israel and join the army. The plan was that she would come back to the U.S. and get her GED which they would have accepted and she could return to Israel.

About six months before her return home, a young man named Nick had recently moved to Florida from St. Louis to join his dad who was attending the congregation. Nick started attending regularly and serving in the congregation. When Josie came back she began to attend the congregation regularly, getting involved with the young adults group, and eventually went through the next Beit Moreshet program. So did Nick. As of this writing they have been married eleven years, and have three beautiful children and they serve in the congregation. So far, Josie has not gone back to Israel!

When I look back on some of these stories, those of my life and the people that God has intertwined with mine, it is obvious in retrospect how His hand is always at work. Josie's story is a great example. Out of the disappointment of not being able to start university right away in Israel, she meets the man that God chose for her, and the result is an incredibly blessed life. So true is the verse: "God causes all things to work together for the good of those that love Him and are called according to His purpose" (Romans 8:28).

CHAPTER 24
RESTORING BROKEN FOUNDATIONS

After that dramatic encounter with the Holy Spirit, we continued to stay in touch with our friends, Alyosha and Jody. They started a small fellowship in Ormond Beach, about three hours up the coast of Florida from where we live. We would drive up and visit them with our kids who got to be friends with theirs. They told us about a couple that they had become friends with, a pastor and his wife, who were also ministers in a work called Restoring the Foundations (RTF), a ministry that helps people heal from past wounds and hurts. They recommended that we look into it, which we did.

We decided to go through the program, which required us to spend five days up in Daytona Beach meeting one on one with the ministering couple. Most of the sessions were individual, each of us meeting separately with the couple for five three-hour sessions. Then we finished with a joint session at the end.

We had no idea what to expect going in. We just knew we needed healing we weren't even sure from what. But God knew. Going through this intensive was not easy, but it was life-changing, and more than anything else we had experienced. We each became aware of the hurts and wounds of our childhoods, and how they affected our present. For me, I realized that my parents' divorce had affected me more than I thought, creating wounds of abandonment and fear of loss, as well as passivity. This was evident when people left the congregation. It was like pouring salt on that unhealed wound of rejection—and I didn't even know it. Lies would roll around in my mind, about not being good enough, or anxiety that people I loved would leave me. For Gloria, having been sexually abused by trusted family members at such an early age, her own set of wounds and hurts created a filter for how she experienced life. We both received a lot of healing that week, but as we were to realize later, there was much more that was needed.

For now, this first time with RTF was incredibly impactful, and helped in all areas: our marriage, our relationship with our children, and our relationships in the congregation. It would be years later that RTF would come back into our lives and dramatically alter our course.

CHAPTER 25
REACHING THE NATIONS

In the year 2000, a young Jewish girl named Melissa found her way into the congregation. She had been raised by now divorced parents in a Hindu cult, at an *ashram* or Hindu religious retreat. Somehow she had found Yeshua, then found us, and started coming to the congregation. She was about three or four years older than Josie, and we kind of adopted her into our family. She spent a lot of time in our home, and became a built-in babysitter, which was great for us as we would travel overseas from time to time. After a couple of years, her dad, Jeff, also became a believer in Yeshua, and began to attend the congregation with his wife.

The annual UMJC conference happened to be in Colorado that year. Melissa went, and while attending the sessions for young adults, she met a young man named Isaac. Isaac and his parents, who were Japanese, lived in northern Virginia and attended a Messianic congregation there. His dad, Paul, worked in the Japanese embassy in Washington, D.C. He was an elder in the congregation there, and I had met him in previous leadership meetings.

Wanting to be closer to Melissa, Isaac decided to move to Florida and join our congregation. He then asked if I would mentor him, which I was happy to do. When his father retired from the embassy job, he decided to move to Florida and join us as well. They became active members of the congregation.

Isaac got a job requiring some overseas travel. Returning from a trip overseas, he got flagged at U.S. immigration. What was the problem? When Isaac was in high school he went through a rebellious phase and had gotten into drugs. He was arrested for possession of drugs and in the process of the case he negotiated with the prosecution a deal whereby he would plead guilty to a felony in exchange for staying out of jail. Another factor was that Isaac was born in Japan. His parents came to the U.S. when he was six months old, so for all practical purposes he was American. However, the family never became citizens; they just had green cards. In the post 9/11 world, they were enforcing the ban on convicted felons of non-citizens in the U.S. Isaac was finally allowed in the country but only after setting a hearing in front of a judge to determine his eligibility to stay in the country.

Around the same time, Isaac had asked Melissa for her hand in marriage and a wedding date was set. We believed that this immigration issue would get resolved. Isaac had a lawyer, and the fact that he had grown up in the States and had a job and was a good citizen would rule the day in his case. After the initial hearing, he was given some time to prepare for a full hearing on his status. In the meantime, plans went on for the wedding. The final hearing was scheduled for a few weeks after the wedding.

Now, the possibility of Isaac having to leave the country became a reality as it got closer to the final hearing. If that were to be the outcome, Isaac and Melissa as newlyweds would have to leave the country and go live in Japan. We had some serious talks about this, and Isaac gave Melissa the option to cancel the wedding, which she refused to do, and was willing to trust God for the outcome. We had a wonderful wedding that I led, with Paul translating into Japanese.

Much prayer had gone into the hearing, asking God for the judge to grant mercy to allow Isaac to stay in the country. However, that's not what happened. The best deal he was offered was that he could voluntarily leave the country, with the possibility of returning in the future. However, if he didn't accept the offer, he would be deported and he could never legally return. We were all heartbroken over this reality that they were going to have to leave the country.

What a shock for Melissa to have to go to a foreign country, with a completely different culture and language! It seemed like an impossible assignment. *How could you, God?* would have been the natural reaction. But as in so many instances, He has plans that we do not know, or are not clear at the time. Here was another reminder of Romans 8:28: "We know that in all things, God works for the good of those who love Him." It didn't seem good at the time for them, or for us because we were losing them. But God works all things for good, so we had to trust that God had other plans.

Just after that, Isaac's parents, Paul and Fumi, decided to retire in Japan as well. Shortly thereafter, Paul and Isaac decided to start a Messianic fellowship in Tokyo, and requested to be under the oversight of our congregation in Boca Raton. They named the congregation the same as ours, Ayts Chayim, Tree of LIfe. It would be the first and the only Messianic congregation in Japan, and still is today.

Over the last fifteen years that they have been there, Isaac has grown incredibly, and now leads the congregation along with his dad. He and Melissa have three beautiful children. Gloria and I have been there twice over the years and taught and ministered in the congregation, and we regularly keep up with them. I remain a remote elder in the congregation and am consulted when difficult situations arise.

BRAZIL AND ARGENTINA

In the same year, I was invited to teach in Brazil. The Messianic Jewish Bible Institute (MJBI) had recently been founded by a friend, first in the Ukraine and in Moscow as the Iron Curtain fell, then in Belo Horizonte, a large city in Brazil, and eventually in Buenos Aires, Argentina. I had not been to the locations in Ukraine or Russia, but was invited to go to Belo. This began a long and close relationship with the leadership family of a Messianic congregation there.

The father of the family, who was the founder of the congregation, the Bible school and associated ministries, was Marcelo Guimaraes. Marcelo had been raised as a Christian, but as an adult began to investigate his family background to find out that he was actually Jewish. Thus he started his journey back to his Jewish roots, and then left his lucrative corporate job to start a Messianic fellowship. Along with the congregation, he had a burden to help other Brazilians whose ancestors were victims of the Spanish and Portuguese Inquisitions, and were forced to convert. He would help them do the research into their lineage and, if it turned out that they were of those called *conversos* aka *moranos*, he would help them return to their Jewish roots. He would later go on to establish the only Museum of the Inquisition in the western world.

Marcelo and his family were to be my hosts on this first trip, in the summer of 2000, and I was scheduled to teach in the Bible school. They picked me up from the airport and, meeting them for the first time, I immediately felt a connection in my spirit with them. In the car from the airport they began to share about a concern in another congregation in Vitoria that Marcelo oversees. Vitoria is a coastal city in the southern part of the country. The congregation was led by a woman who was very controlling and manipulative. Marcelo, as the overseer of the congregation, was frustrated in his attempts to resolve ongoing conflicts within that assembly.

As soon as he began describing the situation, my response was that it sounded like she was being influenced by a Jezebel spirit. This controlling spirit is based on the biblical Jezebel, the wife of Ahab, king of Israel. Jezebel was from the Phoenician city of Tyre and a worshiper of idols (1 Kings 16:31). She used control, manipulation and witchcraft in her relationship with her husband, the king, to accomplish her evil and selfish desires. The Jezebel spirit operates in similar fashion today, through control and manipulation over others. Typically, it operates through women, but not always. It is often given free rein due to the passivity of the men around her, either a husband or other male figures. In this case the leader of the congregation was single, and had other women in the role of leadership.

In the Body of Yeshua the role of women in general can spark all kinds of debate. That aside, as Marcelo described the situation, it seemed like a classic case of Jezebel at work. His excited response to me was, "Yes, that is it, thank you! I want to send you there to straighten them out!" That is what I get for opening my big mouth! But I did feel peace in my heart about it, and was willing to go on the adventure.

A few days later, after I had finished the course I taught at the Bible school, I flew to Vitoria, an hour's flight. Vitoria is a beautiful city on the coast with beautiful beaches and surrounding hills. The congregational leader in question and her assistant picked me up from the airport and drove me around town to show me the sights. In my heart, I was continually asking the Lord to show me what I was to do here.

We go to the top of a hill, and there is an ancient cathedral overlooking the city. In the cathedral is a large statue of Mary facing the city. I immediately sensed that this is the ruling spirit over the city. The Bible is clear about making idols or graven images or praying to anyone or anything other than Him. Followers of Yeshua are to have nothing to do with this practice, so this statue in the cathedral was not representing anything godly.

We know that in the spirit realm there are "powers and principalities, and worldly forces of darkness in heavenly places" (Ephesians 6:12). These are demonic forces sent by satan (*satan* come from a Hebrew word meaning "enemy") to cause disruption, confusion, and discord among the followers of Yeshua. These

spiritual forces are particularly active in trying to destroy congregations. This is the battle in the unseen realm that often as
believers in Yeshua we are either not aware of, or forget about, or
dismiss. However, the enemy is relentless and the spirits assigned
to a region are persistent in looking for any opening to wreak
havoc. These demonic forces have a hierarchy. The "principalities" are the higher echelon "officers" that will be assigned to a
city or municipality. In this case, through the discernment of the
Holy Spirit in my heart I sensed that that ruling spirit of this city,
the principality, was of a feminine dominant nature, such as the
Jezebel spirit. The statue of Mary was an important clue to understanding this and confirmed my initial thoughts. Along with that
spirit there is often a spirit of sensuality and promiscuity, which
seemed be prevalent in the culture as well.

After the tour of the city, the ladies hosting me dropped me
off at my hotel to rest and get ready for the Friday night service,
Erev Shabbat. As I sat there thinking and praying about what to do
and how to approach the situation, I opened my Bible and looked
at the weekly Torah portion. Before I did that, I prayed, "Lord,
show me if there is something in this week's Torah portion that
would give me the wisdom I need to address this issue. Let me
see it." I opened my bible to the weekly portion with the idea that
I would share a message based on whatever the portion was. To
my amazement, the first thing I read is where God commands
the children of Israel, that when they enter the Land, they are to
destroy all the Asherah poles that were erected by the Canaanites
(Deuteronomy 7). These poles had carved images to represent the
female goddess Asherah that they worshiped. She was the goddess
of fertility and evoked sexual themes.

I felt that God had given me the answer. So I put together a
message based on this Torah portion and spoke about feminiza-
tion, in terms of power play that can happen in the community
of Yeshua. I spoke of the consequences of such a situation, and

emphasized how important it is for men to step up and be the spiritual leaders. At the end of the message, I gave an invitation for the men of the congregation to come forward, and I prayed over them to become the spiritual leaders in their households and in the congregation.

Of course I knew it would not sit well with the lady leaders. They never said a word as they drove me back to the airport the next morning. When I returned to Belo to be with Marcelo again, he had already received a scathing email about me. He thanked me and said he totally supported me.

Sometime after all this, on a subsequent trip to Brazil, I learned from Marcelo that the congregation in Vitoria continued to have problems, and eventually the leader left. About fifteen years later, Gloria and I were on another visit and it so happened there was a banquet celebration of Marcelo's time in ministry. All the leaders of the various congregations that he had helped start and develop were present. He took me over to a table and introduced me to this group of men. They were the leaders of the congregation in Vitoria. They thanked me for that night and what I shared, and they had since become stronger leaders since the leader with the Jezebel spirit and her "accomplices" had departed from the congregation. It was encouraging to me to see these guys after all the years and to know that something positive had come out of that trip to Vitoria.

In the years that followed, Gloria would accompany me to Brazil for the teaching time, and together we developed strong friendships with Marcelo and his family that continue to this day. After a couple of years of going to Brazil for teaching in the Bible school, another branch of MJBI opened in Buenos Aires, Argentina, and we were invited to teach there as well and became friends with the couple that led it.

CHAPTER 26
THE JOY AND DISAPPOINTMENT IN RELATIONSHIPS

With the many other connections and doors of friendship that God opened for us, I really learned the value of relationships. That, in fact, is His plan and purpose for us. It is to be in relationship with others on a deeper and more intimate level, whether it's those that He brings into the congregation, or those that we meet in our travels. All this was possible because of God's intervention in my life, and my growing intimacy with Him.

The hard part is when people decide, for whatever reason, that they no longer want to be part of the congregation, and leave. This has always been the tough part of the ministry, and over the years there has been this pattern of people getting close and serving, then getting offended over something, and leaving. Often when speaking to those people, we do not have a frank conversation.

One family had been with us for several years. They had come to us in the mid 90s as newlyweds but had separated. We helped them get back together, and they served in the congregation faithfully. The husband, a musician, was active in the worship team. The wife had trouble getting pregnant, so we prayed earnestly with them and after a while the wife was pregnant and had twins, a boy and a girl. We had the circumcision on our dining room table in our house, as we did for several baby boys that were born in our congregation.

Then one day the couple met with us to tell us that they felt it was time for them to move on, that God was calling them out. But what we believed to be the reason was that the husband was offended that he had been overlooked in a leadership position in the congregation, and that a younger man who had not been in the congregation as long as he had been chosen. Now that same sense of loss and abandonment was coming upon me again. It would be easy in those situations to feel like, *After all I've done for you and this is what I get!* I resisted going down that road, but a part of me did feel pulled that way.

One of the hard lessons that these hurtful incidents taught me was about holding things too tightly. Corrie Ten Boom, the Dutch woman that survived the death camp at Ravensbrück, would say that we have to always hold people and things loosely. If we hold them too tight, God may have to pry our fingers off of them. This has been such a hard lesson, yet so true for me in these thirty-two years of working with people. The challenge remains to allow His mercy to flow through me, even when people behave poorly, get offended and angry, and leave without being transparent. Each time that happened over the years, I had to resist that feeling of abandonment and being victimized. I eventually overcame this through God's mercy, love and healing.

In the meantime, there were more hurtful and difficult situations in our relationships with folks into whom we'd poured our lives. At some point we had a simple revelation, "Hurt people, hurt people." It would be easy to say that it was "those people" but that would just be perpetuating the victim mentality that is so easy to fall into. The adage applies both ways! We too were hurt people hurting other people, while blaming them and not seeing our part. The flip side of that, and the good news, is that healed people, heal people. That is God's desire and ours too!

It was around 1995 that a Christian woman, Carol, started to attend the congregation. She told us about her Jewish husband. They both had a background of addiction but were now sober and active in AA. He was far from believing in Yeshua and had no interest in joining her at the congregation. We committed to pray for Gary.

After about a year, he came to a Hanukkah event, during which we had the usual white elephant gift exchange we do every year. Gary participated, and there was one gift that he kept looking at and picking up, then going back to, and he finally chose it. Turns out it was a New Testament Bible! He would later say that something drew him to that particular gift. He then started to actually read the Bible for the first time, and the following year on Christmas day, which ironically fell on a Shabbat that year, he received Yeshua as his Messiah. Gary and Carol began to serve faithfully in the congregation together.

Fast forward about twenty years and they started to have marital problems. We tried to help, but it seemed hopeless as they each were hurt and getting further and further apart. Sadly, they got divorced. However, five years later, they started to reconnect, and are currently in the process of reconciling and restoring their marriage. While Carol had once stopped coming to the congregation, they are now both back in the congregation together. It has been amazing to see what God is able to do if we are willing to humble ourselves, and take responsibility for our part.

Relationships are complicated things, whether in marriage, family, or friendships. But this is the place where we learn to grow, especially through conflict and disappointment. It is God's design that we be in relationship because it is through those relationships, especially the close ones, that we learn about ourselves and have the opportunity to grow, to love and be loved, even though we run the risk of hurt and disappointment.

THE HOUSE OF BREAD

As part of our connection to Tikkun, we would attend a conference every year. At one of those conferences, we received a prophetic word that has proven to be accurate over the years. We do believe that God speaks in different ways to us. The Bible is the most common way, since we believe that every word is inspired by Him as a guide for living according to His design. There are times when a verse or passage that I have read many times before, jumps out of the page. It's the Holy Spirit illuminating it in a way that I had not seen before. God also speaks through words of encouragement from others to strengthen us.

At this particular conference, we had a word of encouragement in the form of a picture. It was picket fence in front of our house. In that picture we were putting loaves of bread on the fence, and people would come and take the bread when we were not looking, or in the house. The interpretation of that picture, or vision, was that the bread represents the Word of God, and that even the people we do not see, or people that have come and gone, have received God's love and encouragement from us through His Word. That vision has been a great comfort during the difficult times— that, no matter how people receive it, our job is to continue to put the "bread" out there, the bread of life, which is the love and healing available through Yeshua.

Around this time there was a young family that came to be with us. The husband was the son of a prominent Messianic leader and the expectation was that he would be mentored under us and become an elder. After a time, it became clear that the couple needed counseling beyond what we could provide. We remembered how helpful Restoring the Foundations (RTF) was for us years earlier, and we looked up who we could send them to for help. We found Mike and Michele in North Florida and called them up to see if they could take this couple for RTF ministry. We sent the couple up there to receive ministry from them. In the course of the conversation with Mike, he was excited to hear that we led a Messianic congregation. He was a lover of Israel and keenly interested in God's plans and purposes for the Jewish people. Mike and Michele would play a pivotal role in our lives later.

As time went on, we continued to have issues with this couple. However, because of our relationship with the man's father, we continued to try to work things out. There was a desire on our part and the father for his son to be made an elder in the congregation. At this point that position was held only by myself and Joshua (not his real name). The elders are the governing board of the congregation, and they are responsible for the spiritual well-being of the members, in addition to constituting the legal board. We had recently lost another elder who had been with us for a long time; he and his wife left over a disagreement. We came to a point where we thought, *Okay, it's time to just bring him in; we need a third elder.*

So we scheduled a time for installing him as an elder but, as a matter of protocol, we announced our intention to the congregation, and invited any feedback. Since there were a couple of negative responses, we decided to put the installation on hold. Well, that started a firestorm from the parents and the couple themselves, and they finally decided to leave the congregation. The greatest show of betrayal came from the father, who had initially disagreed with his son's decision to resign from the congregation, but now wanted to throw us under the bus. It was another difficult episode that once again brought up the old lies and wounds of abandonment, and played into the enemy's strategy of divide and rule.

Relationships are difficult for most of us. We learn from a young age how to function in relationships by what is modeled to us in our home growing up—good or bad. For me, as a product of divorced parents, and having been divorced myself, I had no healthy model of a marriage relationship. This lack of a healthy experience with marriage affected all my relationships, especially those in leadership in a congregation. I have come to see that healthy leaders produce healthy relationships, and the opposite is true as well. The challenge in relationships is that God designed us to be in relationships from friendships to the most intimate one, marriage.

Over time, I learned that people who come into a congregation will tend to bring the dynamics of their family of origin into the spiritual family. And that includes the leader. So every time someone left, or there was conflict in the congregation, that fear of conflict and abandonment would kick in. It wasn't until later that I would be able to see beyond my experience and continue the process of deep healing from past wounds.

CHAPTER 27
FORTY YEARS

In August, 2022, Gloria and I celebrated our fortieth wedding anniversary. In looking back over those forty years, it is obvious that the hand of God has guided us and been with us even when we did not know Him. From those early days of drinking and drugging, to going through treatment and being part of AA and Alanon, to the faith journey, to having three great kids, to being called into full time ministry with all the challenges and disappointments and blessings, He has been with us. It really is a miracle that we have made it together after forty years, and are more in love today than ever.

There was a time early in the marriage where we had major problems. Even though we became believers in Yeshua, our conflicts and struggles did not go away. In fact, they seemed to have spilled over into our relationship. When your mother tells your wife to leave and go back to her parents' house, you know it's bad. Fortunately for us, Gloria did not take that advice and stuck it out.

When we moved to Colorado Springs, we thought the financial situation would change and it did—it actually got worse! When the "pie in the sky" from my real estate friend turned out to be just that, and I finally came to understand that God had other purposes for me, we sought the counsel of a Christian counselor for our marriage. In a few sessions he opened the Bible and went through the basics of our different roles as husband and wife.

This was new to both of us. For Gloria, her mom was in charge, and even laid out her dad's clothes every day. That was her model which she imitated. For me, although coming from divorced parents, my mom was also the dominant one, and Dad was somewhat emotionally disconnected.

The good thing is that we began to implement some important biblical principles in our marriage. The biggest was the fact that as the husband, I am responsible to God for the marriage. I am to be the spiritual leader of the home, and to love Gloria "as Messiah loved the community and gave Himself up for her" (Ephesians 5:25). That was a heavy order, which continues to challenge me every day. For Gloria, it was the news that she wasn't in charge, and that her role was to "submit to your husband as to the Lord"(Ephesians 5:22). Neither one of us knew what either of these words fully meant, but we at least had a framework to move forward in our marriage based on the foundation of God's Word.

To be honest, this idea of "loving your wife as Messiah loved the community and gave Himself up for her" definitely challenged my human mind. But as I surrendered myself to God's way, I began to understand what love actually is. The biblical idea of love is totally different than what is seen in the movies or romantic novels. Rather than be governed by emotions or feelings, that love is intentional and involves sacrifice, of giving to another regardless of the cost. The best-known verse in the New Testament probably says it all: "For God so loved the world that He gave His only Son that whoever believes in Him would not perish but have eternal life" (John 3:16). This is the model of love. Love is action, not a feeling.

I remember one morning during my daily devotion asking God how I could love Gloria when we were having so much conflict and how different we were. He asked me this question: "Would you be willing to let Me love her through you?" I was still pretty young in my faith at this time, but I knew enough to know that when God asks you a question like that, He does expect a certain answer. Of course, I said, "Yes." I came to understand that, unless we love with God's kind of love, it will always be fleeting and fickle. But God's love is unconditional and sacrificial.

So I began to look for ways to serve and honor my wife. I certainly was not perfect at it, and I still am not. Along the way we learned about "love languages." We all have different love languages, or ways that we receive love. For Gloria, her main love language is acts of service. I discovered that there were certain things that really bugged her, like leaving socks on the floor, not making the bed, and so on. So even with the little acts of service that I was able to do, allowing God to love her through me, my perspectives began to change. I was beginning to understand what God's love really is.

Another important aspect of His love is that I cannot properly love Gloria or others unless I am able to receive His love for myself. The more I open my heart to His love, the love of the Father, the more I am able to share that love with others. His love is literally endless, infinite. The only way that I can have a continuous flow of His love is by spending time every day in His Word and in His presence. I have found though that there are blocks and hindrances to our ability to receive His love and that usually goes back to our childhood wounds and hurts that are unhealed.

And as you already know, we both came into the marriage with lots of baggage. Gloria grew up going to church every Sunday morning, Sunday night, and Wednesday night. In addition, she was in youth groups learning "sword drills" which were games designed to learn the Bible. She knew Scripture, yet what she experienced in her biological family did not line up with who God really is and what He intended. Besides being sexually abused by extended family members, her home life with her parents and siblings was not great.

Her Mom, Bonnie, ruled the roost out of her own hurts and wounds, and, most likely, was also sexually abused. She was sick a lot, and generally an angry, self-centered person. Gloria's dad, Fred was a sweet, hardworking man that put up with a lot from his wife. Gloria tells the story that her mom was always threatening to leave, often after she had one drink too many. She would walk out ignoring the cries of the children and go down the block, only to return an hour later. After high school, Gloria also started down that same road of drinking and drugging, landing in Estes Park a few years later where our lives intersected.

Gloria is the oldest of four, with two sisters and a brother. Her mom was sick a lot and on medications. She was in and out of hospital with kidney failure and other issues, and she passed away at the young age of 59. We all went to the funeral, and it was the first time that I had been to a "wake" where the casket was open.

Sometime after, Fred remarried and carried on with life. But a few years later he too became ill with cancer. Gloria decided to go visit him. Before Gloria left, she was cleaning the house. While she was vacuuming and thinking about her dad, she heard a voice, presumably the Lord's, say, "Fred is not your daddy." She was shocked and wondered what this could mean. When she got to her dad's she saw he was not doing well under chemo treatment. They decided to go for a ride. All the while she was wondering how to approach the subject, and asked the Lord for a sign. They decided to go visit the cemetery where Bonnie was buried. While looking at the gravestone, there was an image of two wedding rings and the date, January 2, 1954, when they were married was engraved on the headstone.

That was Gloria's signal to broach the subject with him, because she was born on July 27, 1954, and realized that she was conceived before her parents were married. So she asked her dad, "Are you my real Daddy?" His answer was vague enough for her to know that what she'd heard that day while housecleaning was preparation for her to know the truth. His answer, "I've always been your daddy." On a visit to her grandmother, it was confirmed that indeed Fred was not her biological father.

Bonnie had joined the military at a young age, and presumably had become pregnant, came home after her service, and married Fred, who would have known that she was pregnant by someone else. Why is this important? For Gloria, this was another step in her healing process in knowing that, regardless of who her biological father was, she had a heavenly Father who loved and cared for her just as she was.

As we exchanged rings on our wedding day, little did we know how much of our past hurts and wounds we still carried. The reality was that neither of us even knew what love was, let alone have the capacity to share that love with another.

At our fifth wedding anniversary we decided to dedicate our marriage to God. Both of us were by now believers in Yeshua, and we had been through a rough first five years of marriage. So we asked our spiritual father, Eliezer, to come and perform a wedding ceremony under the *chupah*, the tradition Jewish wedding canopy. The chupah represents the covering of God over the couple, something we definitely did not have in our first wedding. We exchanged our vows again, this time acknowledging and thanking God for bringing us together. It was a wonderful time with the folks from the congregation in Colorado Springs joining us.

Over the forty years of our marriage God has been so faithful. Through all our hardships and disappointments, both in our relationship and in the work of the ministry, we have seen God's faithfulness and blessings at every turn. He blessed us with three wonderful children, Josie, Micha and Avi, in addition to Sammi and Seth from my first marriage. They all love each other and have grown up to be good and loving people.

Sammi and David went on to have three more children after Jordan. Joshua and Joseph were born while they still lived in

Florida, and Kaylee was born after they moved back to Colorado. All four of them are young adults today and we maintain good relationships as we visit Colorado usually once a year.

After high school Seth went on to college and had a keen interest in the Spanish language and eventually would speak it fluently. After joining the Peace Corps after college he served in Bolivia for several years, then moved back to the States and lived with us for a short time. Then he got a job in Ecuador managing a large rose farm. We had the privilege of visiting him while he was there. After about five years he came back and settled in Miami. In 2019, after we had come back from Israel and we were preparing for our family Passover seder, he asked if he could bring a "friend" to the seder. He had brought others in the past, but Marianna was different. As a Montessori school teacher she was immediately embraced by our three young grandchildren, Tirzah, Noa and Shiloh, who was a baby at the time. We all really liked her.

Apparently so did Seth, because a couple of months later we were sent a photo of an ultrasound, showing a baby. It was a bit of a shock, but we were happy for them, and although there was no talk of marriage, they were committed to the relationship and made plans to move in together and prepare to be parents. The baby was due in the first week of January 2020 and we soon found out that it was a boy. One day at the end of December we got a call from Seth saying they were at the hospital. Marianna had thought that she was going into labor but when they got to the hospital the doctor could not find a heartbeat and it appeared that the baby had died in utero. We rushed down to the hospital to be with them and they were prepping Mariana for a C-section, but the baby was lifeless. They had named him Gabriel after my grandfather.

It was a sad and traumatic event that could have driven them apart. We were all heartbroken. However it was just a few weeks later that Covid hit, and they locked down together. A few months later we received the news that Marianna was pregnant again, and

Ilan was born on March 31, 2021. God is all about redemption, restoration, and turning our mourning into joy. Ilan is a healthy and active boy and we are so grateful for how it has worked out. He is grandchild number eight. We love and support them, and have a close relationship, and see that they are committed to each other.

Micha, our middle child, started working part time at Starbucks in Boca, while attending Florida Atlantic University. She graduated with a degree in English and a minor in Judaic studies. She then went full time with Starbuck's as a store manager. Shortly after graduating, she moved to Colorado to be with her older sister, Sammi, in Estes Park and continued with Starbuck's there. Then she moved to Denver where she has lived the past ten years. While there, she met the man of her life, a young man named Samuel, and they will be wed on October 1, 2023. We were all very excited for her, and we love Samuel who is from Nigeria.

Avi, our youngest son married Jacquie in 2016. They had known each other since they were seven years old when she and her family came into the congregation. They home-schooled together, then went to Boca High School together serving in the Navy Junior ROTC program. After high school they "announced" that they were in a relationship. Shortly after, Jacquie moved to Richmond, VA to live with friends. Avi followed shortly after and they have been there ever since. After six years of marriage, they had their first baby in September, 2022, a girl named Libi,which is Hebrew for "my heart" She is our ninth grandchild. Such a blessing!

I am incredibly proud of all five children and who they have become. Sammi raised four beautiful children, overcoming the challenges of teenage pregnancy and went on to get her Bachelors and Masters in accounting. She presently works for the city of Longmont. Seth has worked for a large international food company as the Caribbean sales director. He and Marianna live in Miami raising Ilan, and we are blessed to live close to them. Josie and Nick have three incredible children, Tirzah, Noa, and Shiloh.

They live near us in Boca Raton and are active members of the congregation. Josie has made a name for herself in local politics, both as a candidate and a successful campaign manager for local races. Micha has worked for Starbucks for the past ten years as a manager. She has matured and grown and is ready for marriage. Avi has established himself as an audio engineer and travels all over the world working conferences and events. He and Jacquie live in Richmond, VA, and are doing great as new parents.

When I look back on the day we got married and where we are today, we are definitely not the same people. Through all of life's uncertainties and surprises, the one constant is His faithfulness and His love. I made a lot of mistakes, but yet somehow in His great mercy, He has kept us and sustained us throughout the forty years. We raised some great kids, and we continue to grow in our love for each other and for the people that God has placed in our lives.

CHAPTER 28
PASSING THE BATON

In the early 2000s a young family came to the congregation, Joshua and Jessica, with their four small children. They immediately felt at home with the congregation, and began to serve faithfully. We took them under our wing, and I began to mentor Joshua, while Gloria was mentoring Jessica. We also became close friends and spiritual parents to them and their children. Over time, they took on more and more responsibilities in the congregation, including leading the youth group. They were also very much a part of the Beit Moreshet program for the ten-day intensives and youth conferences. I saw great leadership potential in Joshua, and we continued to meet one on one.

The time came after several years where the Lord was speaking to me about the next generation of leadership in our own congregation. While I was not yet ready to retire, I sensed that, to be true to the vision of raising up the next generation, it should apply in my leadership role as well. I felt that Joshua would be the one to pass on the baton to. We approached them about this and they were agreeable, and so we began a two year process of transition, where we continued to meet regularly and he came on staff as assistant Rabbi. We had a list of stipulations that we felt were necessary before we officially turned them over to the congregation.

It was around 2011: the congregation was flourishing, and we had a very robust children's, youth, and young adults groups. Our average attendance was around 100 and there was a lot of enthusiasm for the vision of the congregation. When the congregation was made aware of the transition plan, most were enthusiastic. Some, however, were not, and voted with their feet walking out the door. We just chalked that up to normal reaction to change.

The question then arose, *What would Gloria and I do next?* We sought counsel from our mentor, Gary K., who had been encouraging us in this transition process. The six of us, Joshua and Jessica, Gloria and I, and Gary and his wife, Shirley, met together. At that meeting we sensed the wisdom of the Lord that, as we proceeded with our transition plan for Joshua to become the Rabbi of the congregation, Gloria and I would focus on leading and expanding the Beit Moreshet program. It was still flourishing as a sub ministry under the congregation. Everyone felt good about that decision, and we proceeded with the planning and implementation. The only thing we weren't sure was if the Beit Moreshet program would sustain us financially. So we began to explore other options.

MINISTERING THE RTF PROGRAM

As congregational leaders, we always had a burden to help people, and we remembered the Restoring the Foundations (RTF) couple, Mike and Michele Green, to whom we had directed the other couple for ministry. We began to entertain the idea of becoming RTF ministers and administer the program ourselves. We met with them and they laid out a training program, mostly in the field, as we were still leading the congregation. Thus we embarked on a two year process to become RTF ministers. The hardest part of the process was completing our own healing before we could be released to help others. Although we had gone through the RTF ministry for ourselves back in 2000, this time it was at a much deeper level. It took a tremendous amount of courage, honesty, and vulnerability to really acknowledge our wounds and close the open doors to the enemy so that God could heal us.

So what exactly is RTF? Restoring the Foundations is an approach to inner healing of the hurts and wounds of the past, typically from childhood. It applies biblical principles in a systematic way to bring lasting healing to individuals and to married couples. It is different from counseling or therapy, in that counseling often addresses symptoms of the hurts and brings awareness, but it does little to actually address the root causes. Knowing why you are hurting and talking about it, is a long way from experiencing healing in your spirit, soul, and body. Therapies can be effective to a degree because they address the soulish realm of the mind, will, and emotions, but again secular therapies fall short. By comparison, RTF addresses all levels of wounding, including the spiritual realm, which is really where the entry points to pain are established. As we learned more and more about RTF, we really felt drawn to it. We could see ourselves using this great ministry approach to help people in a way that we had not been able to in the past.

To give some background, Restoring the Foundations was developed by a couple, Chester and Betsy Kylstra, in the 1980s. Chester was a systems engineer at NASA, literally a rocket scientist, and Betsy was a Christian counselor. They had a family and a nice life, and then, while they were in their forties, God called them to go to Bible school. While they were in Bible school, God uploaded this approach to them and they developed it into a systematic (systems engineering) structure that invites the Holy Spirit to bring about complete healing for the person. There are four areas they identified that need to be addressed that are common to us all:

1. **Sins of the Fathers and Resulting Curses** (SOFCs). These are the sin and behavior issues that we tend to inherit from our

parents and grandparents. Common examples are addictions, anger, abuse and many more. We identify these sin and behavior issues, confess and repent of them, and receive God's generational blessings.

2. **Ungodly Beliefs.** These are the lies that we believe about ourselves, about God, and about others. We may not even be aware of them or really understand why we choose to believe them. This process helps bring awareness so we can exchange the lies for His truth that sets us free!

3. **Soul/Spirit Hurts.** These are the hurts and wounds that we have experienced in our own lives generally from childhood. We think they do not affect us because they were so long ago; but that is a lie. Those childhood experiences happened during our formative years, and they are what impact our lives the very most!

4. **Demonic Oppression.** As believers in Yeshua we cannot be "possessed" by the enemy, but we can be and sometimes are "oppressed." This means we can be influenced from the outside, in our dark thoughts and clouded perceptions. The three previous areas are what are called "legal open doors" for the enemy to penetrate, and by addressing and receiving healing in those areas, this last part is relatively simple: the demonic influences now must leave since their legal right has been removed.

As Gloria and I began to learn more and more about this process, we became more excited to think about the possibilities of helping people in ways that we had never been able to in the past. Now we could have an understanding of how to get to the root issues that had never been addressed.

For parts of our training we would drive up to Hendersonville, North Carolina, where RTF had its international training center. There we met some incredible people, and the leadership was very excited that we showed up, as they had not had any Jewish believers that were part of the RTF network yet.

In one of the early sessions, we were learning about one of the core issues related to shame. We were looking at how shame entered into the human race when Adam and Eve sinned by eating the fruit from the tree that God told them not to. Genesis 2:25 tells us that in the beginning they "were naked and unashamed." Then in the next chapter we have the serpent, satan himself, who, out of his jealousy of God's new family, tempts them through lies to eat of the tree of the Knowledge of Good and Evil. The very moment they ate, it says that they "saw that they were naked and they hid" (Genesis 3). All of a sudden they were ashamed, and they took fig leaves to cover themselves. They tried to fix their situation on their own, to control the consequences, so to speak, so that they would not be "found out." This became their false identity, one based on shame as opposed to how God created them: His son and daughter, to be "fruitful and multiply and subdue the earth." They were God's representatives in this physical world embodying His image and likeness.

As I heard this teaching I began to think about Israel and God's calling and purpose for her as a nation. He gave her an identity, as His "first born son" (Exodus 4:33; Hosea 10:1). After he called them out of Egypt with great miracles—even destroying the greatest army on the earth at the time—He declared that they were His "treasured possession" and also a "kingdom of priests" (Exodus 19). This describes their identity and purpose. However, it was not too long after they entered the Promised Land that they rebelled, and as a result, God sent the prophets to warn them to turn back to Him or they would suffer the consequences, which ultimately was exile from the Land. As exiles in foreign lands they would be shamed and scorned.

So in that moment I realized that, just as this shame-based identity applies to individuals, it also applied to the nation of

Israel. We have taken on a shame-based identity in being dispersed among the nations. However, despite our rebellion and disobedience, there was always the promise of restoration of our true identity and purpose. The restoration is two-fold: the first is the re-gathering back to the Land which happened over the past 100 plus years, culminating in Israel becoming a sovereign independent nation in 1948. But there is also the promise of spiritual restoration, of which the Messianic movement of Jewish people turning to Yeshua is the beginning.

As this hit me, I began to weep. I was asked to share what this all meant as a Jewish believer in Yeshua, and I shared this piece about Israel and her identity. The folks there received it and it was a great blessing for all of us.

I have come to understand the supreme importance of our God-given identity that was lost in the garden of Eden. He formed us and knew us before we were born, and that He has a plan and purposes for each of us. But we have an enemy that is on the prowl to rob us of that identity and purpose, even as followers of Yeshua. Now, as followers of Yeshua, we no longer have to live in shame, fear and guilt. He has adopted us and calls us His sons and daughters. We are "co-heirs" with Messiah (Romans 8:17), His Son.

As we continued with the transition of leadership in the congregation, Gloria and I completed our training to become RTF ministers. As part of our training we were required to once again to go through the "Thorough Format" ministry to receive further healing. While we had gone through the ministry back in 2000 and received wonderful healing, this time there was an even deeper level of healing that God had in store for us. as there were still many things in our individual lives and in our marriage that we recognized needed further healing. This Thorough Format ministry consisted of five three-hour individual sessions for each of us, and two couple sessions, one at the beginning of the sessions and one at the end. That final couple session was very powerful, as we were able to share with each other how some of the negative experiences and the resulting lies that we brought into the marriage had affected the relationship. We asked for forgiveness for those things and for allowing them to affect our marriage, then we share the truths that God had revealed to us during our individual sessions. This was an incredibly powerful time of learning how to communicate from a place of wholeness and healing, not from a place of neediness and defensiveness.

How many marriages fail because of these issues, where one or both spouses are operating out of the hurts of the past and not even realizing how these hurts affect the marriage! Maybe that is you in your marriage.

For me, the shame and fear of abandonment that had affected our marriage and most of my life was gone. As I began to really see who I am, that my identity is who God says I am, and not based on the lies that I was believing, it made an incredible difference in my relationship with God and with others. Having gone through this ministry for ourselves, we are so much better equipped to help other couples.

On September 14, 2014, we had a great celebration in the congregation when Joshua was officially ordained as our new Rabbi. Gloria and I had spent the previous one to two years developing the ministry which we re-named Heritage House, the English translation of Beit Moreshet. I remained as an elder in the congregation and we attended whenever we were in town.

CHAPTER 29
OUR NEW ADVENTURES

I am convinced that God has written in His heavenly books a destiny and calling for every individual born. This is a hard concept to wrap our minds around, especially if we are going through a hard time, or disappointment or hardship. However, there is the reality of God's love that supersedes all our hurts, fears, and traumas.

God tells us in His Word that He IS love. It's not just the essence of His nature and character; it's who He is. Because He is love, He is inherently good, and desires good things for us. At the same time, we have an enemy, a thief, who also has a destiny in mind for us. His plan is to thwart and sabotage that destiny that God has planned for us.

In our new ministry season as RTF leaders, we started to travel quite a bit. At first it was just within the U.S. but eventually we would go to Brazil, Japan, and Israel and present the RTF workshop in congregations and with individuals. In Brazil, we presented the workshop with a translator to about 500 people at a congregation led by our friends in Belo Horizonte, where I had taught at their Bible School many years ago.

It was incredibly exciting to see God move in such a mighty way in such a large group, even through a translator. Many of those attending received great inner healing from Him. Because of the sensual nature of the culture in Brazil, many who attended were suffering because of sexual brokenness, either because of abuse, or promiscuity or typically both. At one point, we asked for those who had suffered because of sexual issues to stand up, and nearly half the congregation did. As we prayed, we sensed that tremendous healing was taking place all over the hall. Sexual brokenness and trauma is not just an issue in Brazil, but is universal. Gloria's experience of having been sexually abused in childhood, and the promiscuity that controlled us in the early years, together with the subsequent healing and restoration through the RTF, gives us firsthand experience of these issues. We can empathize and minister to those who have been through similar experiences. In the years that we have been working with the RTF, we see this as a very common damage to the soul that only God can bring someone through in this healing process. Man's methods always fall short, but God's healing plan works every time!

RTF IN ISRAEL

We began to have the burden to go to Israel and bring RTF there. There are RTF ministers in many countries around the world; but there were none in Israel at the time. We started exploring opportunities by sending out letters of introduction to several ministry leaders in the land, some of whom we were friends with and others we did not know. In the letters we shared a little about ourselves as Messianic leaders, trained in the RTF approach to healing. We offered to come and present the ministry.

One of the responses we received was from a pastor of a mostly Russian-speaking Messianic congregation. He referred us to a couple, Igor and Naomi, who are elders in the congregation that do all the counseling and family ministry. Igor is from Ukraine, and Naomi is British. She wrote to us how, when she lived in Ukraine, an RTF couple had come to her church, and so she was familiar with the ministry and was eager to have us come. The congregation was in Ashdod, a city in the southern part of Israel on the coast. We could see God's hand in this and agreed to visit on our first trip, which was about three weeks long, longer than any other prior trip. In subsequent trips we would stay six to ten weeks at a time.

We became close friends with Igor and Naomi and the congregation in Ashdod. Naomi was fluent in Russian, having lived in Russia and the Ukraine and also studying Russian in school. She was able to translate when we spoke to the congregation as well as to Igor, who did not speak English, just Russian and some Hebrew.

On the first trip we presented a two-hour seminar on Shame/ Fear/Control. The congregation was very enthusiastic as people began experiencing breakthroughs, and we also did a couple of three-hour individual healing sessions with folks in the congregation. The impact was undeniable, and they were eager to have us come back for more ministry, which we did over the next couple of years.

All the while we were getting closer to Naomi and Igor and their children as friends, and we learned about their amazing story. Igor had been married before in Ukraine with five children. When the Iron Curtain fell from the Soviet Union in the early 1990s, Igor and his family made plans to make Aliyah. A month before they were to move to Israel, they had a terrible automobile accident and his wife was killed. Igor decided to go anyway, and he and his five children began to make a life in Israel. A few years later, Naomi went to Israel to visit friends she knew in Ukraine who moved to Israel, and they introduced her to Igor. The two fell in love and got married. She helped raise the children, and they also had two of their own, and girl and a boy. Each time we went to Israel over the next few years, we would spend a lot of time with them, and trained them together with a group of ten people from the congregation.

The goal was to train a team to be able to do what we call an "issue focus session" which is a three-hour session covering one issue that the person may be struggling with. In order to effectively carry out this training, which is pretty intense even in English, we had to have all our materials translated into Russian. We were able to get that done, and on one of our trips to Israel we spent two full weekends going through the training with the team. The language situation made it difficult. In this type of training, they practice the ministry steps on each other, with us observing, to make sure they understand and are doing it correctly. We also separate the men and the women, which meant having a men's translator for me and a women's translator for Gloria. It was difficult, but very exciting to bring this wonderful ministry, that we so fully believed in, to this group in Israel—the first one of its kind.

After that trip, those who successfully completed the ministry training were able to start working and helping others in the congregation. To this day, we still keep in touch with Igor and Naomi as the team leaders, and they keep us updated on the progress of the team.

On subsequent trips to Israel, we were welcomed in various Messianic congregations and churches to present RTF workshops. We had our materials translated into Hebrew, Russian, and Arabic. One of the highlights of the last time we were there was doing a conference organized by two Arab churches at a hotel. In addition, we had many opportunities to meet with individuals and couples for Issue Focused three-hour sessions, and the Thorough Format Ministry Program. We were so humbled and excited to be used by God to bring healing and hope to Jews and Arabs in the land of Israel!

Over our thirty years of walking our faith journey, we met many leaders in Israel who became friends. We also had the opportunity to go to places and meet people we otherwise would never have met. On each trip to Israel, we would usually get in touch with my cousins on my mother's side, Menachem and Yossi, and their wives as well. While they were not so much interested in our faith and the reason we were in the country, they were always gracious and hospitable whenever we would meet.

On two occasions we were in Israel for historical events. One was the 70th year anniversary of Israel's independence in 2018. This was an incredible time of celebration, fireworks, dancing in the streets and more. That same year was the other historical occasion. It was the official move of the U.S. Embassy from Tel Aviv to Jerusalem at the direction of then President Trump. Congress passed it and then President Clinton passed a resolution back in the 90s recognizing Jerusalem as the capital of the Jewish state of Israel. However, it did not become a reality until President Trump implemented it twenty years later. While we weren't at the actual ceremony in Jerusalem on May 14, 2018, when the event took place, we were in the country, and had been in Jerusalem just a couple of days before. All over Jerusalem were banners reading: "President Trump, Making Israel Great Again!" It was as exciting a moment for us as it was for the nation of Israel.

Our last trip to Israel was in 2019 before COVID changed the world. We were there for ten weeks mostly doing RTF workshops and meeting with people individually for personal ministry. As always, we spent time with our friends, Igor and Naomi and their children. We were planning to go back in 2020 for 8 weeks and had already booked our flights, and for the first time had our schedule of workshops set in place. Shortly after we got home from the 2019 trip, we got the news that Naomi was diagnosed with pancreatic cancer. It was shocking and sad for us to hear, as she was barely forty years old at the time, and in great physical condition as a runner. However, we were all confident that she would overcome the cancer. Sadly, she passed away after nearly two years of treatments.

There was also a long-term friendship with Jackie and Eddie. We first met them when they came to visit family in South Florida in the early 90s. Shortly after that they made Aliyah and were involved in ministry, which included helping to plant a Messianic congregation in Jerusalem. On all the trips we took to Israel, we always stayed for part of the time with them. It was very special spending time with some of our best friends and sharing life together. Eddie developed a brain tumor and had various treatments, but in the end, it took his life shortly after we returned from Israel on our last visit in 2019. It was a great loss for the many people whose lives he had touched through his ministry, including Gloria and me.

Our time in Israel was always special because of the relationships that we have built over the years, as well as feeling that sense of being "home" in the Land. On every trip we would visit new historical sites and were always awed by the historical and spiritual connection of our people to the Land.

With all the opportunities that God has placed in front of us, I am continually reminded of the encouraging word that we received years before about putting out the bread. We are still putting out the "bread." Some we see taking it, and some are coming and taking it when we are not "looking." In other words, more and more do we understand our role, which is to share our own experiences, including the hard parts, and to impart God's love which is stronger than any of our hurts and wounds. If He can do what He did for us, He can do it for anyone. If He could take a hurt, wounded girl from a small town in Mississippi, and an arrogant, stubborn Jew from NY, and bring His love and healing to them, He can do it for anyone!

In July, 2020 in the midst of COVID, Joshua decided to step down unexpectedly. So I stepped back in as the Rabbi of the congregation, which we had renamed "Shalom Boca." It certainly was not what I had planned. But once again, God had other ideas and plans. We were perfectly content with our lives of travel and sharing the blessing of Restoring the Foundations in congregations, and with married couples and individuals.

So now it was congregational leader 2.0. Soon after this "re-transition" to Rabbi of the congregation, when in prayer I heard God say, "You got this!" I was at peace, and continue to lead the congregation to this day with the help of great people that God has knitted together.

CHAPTER 30

GENERATION TO GENERATION

In Judaism there is an emphasis on *dor l'dor*, meaning "generation to generation." This important principle comes from the Torah, where over and over we read that God told the children of Israel to teach their children and to pass on the stories of His miracles and wonders that He has done for His people. This is exemplified in the traditional prayer of the *Shema* and the *V'ahavta*, taken from Deuteronomy 6:4-7.These are the first prayers learned by Jewish children and are recited daily by religious Jews.

In part it says:

> "Hear O Israel, the Lord our God, the Lord is one.
> Love ADONAI your God with all your heart and with all your soul and with all your strength. These words, which I am commanding you today, are to be on your heart. You are to **teach them diligently to your children** and speak of them when you sit in your house, when you walk by the way, when you lie down and when you rise up" (emphasis added).

Additionally, in the account of the first Passover in the book of Exodus, it is written that every year when we celebrate the holiday of Passover we are to be sure to tell our children the story of God's miraculous deliverance of His people from slavery. When I was growing up, Passover was always a highlight of the year for me. Since I had gone to religious school and knew the Hebrew, my grandfathers always had me read and participate in the telling of the story. The traditional book that is read during the Passover seder meal is called a *Haggadah*, which means "telling." We would have seder the first night with my dad's family, and the second night with my mom's family. My dad's family was far more fun, as there were more cousins, and my grandmother made a special raisin wine for us kids. At Passover, the tradition is to have four cups of wine that are drunk throughout the seder as we go through the Haggadah. We kids drank the raisin wine and by the end of the night we all were acting pretty silly, almost "drunk." It was not until years later that I came to find out that there was no alcohol in that raisin wine, but that we were "drunk" because of the sugar content. However, these seders created wonderful memories of family, and the feeling of a special bond with my grandfathers and the generations that went before me.

This idea of passing things on from generation to generation is so important on many levels. For me, personally, it's just knowing that I am not an island, that my story didn't just start when I was born, but started way before me. It was impacted by my family escaping the Nazis, and Rabbi Chayut way back in the 1600s, and his great grandfather escaping Portugal; and ultimately it went back to the Hebrew slaves God freed from Egypt. All of us have a story that began generations ago, all the way back to a garden where God and man walked together. What is more exciting is that I get to pass on these stories and experiences that become a part of the journey of my children and their children for generations to come.

As parents, we choose what we pass down. Instead of passing down our brokenness, we do the work of passing on healing and live the story of God's faithfulness, His love and His mercy throughout all the generations.

As it is written:

"Great is ADONAI, and greatly to be praised—His greatness is unsearchable. One generation will praise Your works to another and declare Your mighty acts" (Psalm 145:3-4 TLV).

In raising our children, we always emphasized the importance of our history and heritage as a people. I am so grateful that God gave Gloria to me because, among other things, she received the revelation of God's eternal plan and purposes for the Jewish people early on. Even with her Southern Baptist upbringing, she would always say, "If God keeps His promise to Israel for all this time, He will keep His promise to me!"

This unity of vision that our children received from us inspired Josie to want to go off to Israel after high school. To this day they all celebrate the feasts, Passover especially, as the yearly reminder of God's goodness and mercy to our people. More than that, we also remember the greater freedom that Yeshua brought at His last Passover, when He laid His life down as the ultimate Passover lamb, the Lamb of God who takes away our sin. This is the most important story of all the stories that I want to pass on to the next generations, not just to my children and my family, but to people everywhere. This is the story of redemption, the story of how God can take an arrogant selfish guy like me, from a broken family, living a life of lawlessness and rebellion, and bring healing and hope, and a life committed to serving others. If He can save and heal my life, He can save and heal anyone, no matter what your life has been like.

Yes, before you were even born, God had a plan to bring you into His great redemption story. He writes our names in His book, with His identity, His purpose, and destiny for our lives. At the same time, there is an enemy who is also right there telling another story, with an identity and purpose to give us as well. His identity for us is to live a life of shame, brokenness, and fear. He wants to separate us from God just like he did with Adam. Out of a shame-based identity, we believe lies such as "I'm a failure," "I'm unloved," "I'm ugly," "I'm not worthy." Living in the wrong identity, and believing the wrong story, thwarts the divine destiny and purpose God has for our lives.

But God has a plan to restore, renew, and redeem us from that old, shame-based life so that we can live the life that He originally intended for us. This is a life filled with joy, peace, and purpose. It is a life modeled after our Master, who sacrificed Himself for us, and gave us an example of how to live. It is a life based on our Designer's intent. This is the life that I want to pass down to my children and grandchildren, so that they too can fulfill the calling and destiny that God has written for them in His book.

For me, this idea of generations has impacted me greatly. There was a legacy of faith, a seed planted, that was left for me that has sprouted into a true tree of life that has born much fruit. We were created to bear fruit, and even if we see ourselves as barren, dry, of no value, God sees us differently. He created you for a purpose— you are not here by accident.

WHAT'S YOUR STORY?

I don't know where your journey started or where you are on your journey now. Whatever your story, even if it is full of disappointment and hardship, God can use those things for your good and the good of others. The key is to let go of control, and to trust that He is a good God who wants good things for us. When I finally gave up the fear and control, He filled me with His peace. It starts with the understanding that because God so loved us, He provided the way out of the darkness and disappointments. That way is through Yeshua, Jesus. It doesn't matter if you are Jewish or not because He is no respecter of persons. He extends the invitation of His love to any who will receive it.

As you have read my story, you can see that He has changed my life the very moment that Yom Kippur night when I finally surrendered to Him. At that moment, my journey took a dramatic change in direction that has led to an incredibly fulfilling life of serving others, raising a family, traveling to places I probably would not have seen otherwise, and making incredible friends around the world. I do not know where my life would be today without Yeshua. Looking back over these last thirty-eight years of following Him, the greatest blessing, besides knowing my identity as His beloved son and having a great wife and kids, is the spiritual family that He has given me.

When I reflect on the incredible stories of some of my ancestors I shared earlier in this book, I am amazed to see how the hand of God has been there throughout all our generations to this moment. On top of that, I recently learned I had family that I didn't know about—a sister named Nancy. This news added to my sense of belonging and purpose, combined with my purpose for the hundreds, if not thousands of other "family" members that God has brought into our lives. These are the people we have had the privilege of sharing God's love with—the "bread" that was taken off the fence—even if we did not see or know the impact it had on their lives. Many have come and gone, and many have come and stayed.

Disappointment, loss, and heartache are part of the human experience. And even if the challenges and hardships that come our way are not of our own choosing, I have learned and experienced the goodness of God, His grace and mercy, and His victory in my life. I see the fruit of the work that He has entrusted to us, both through the leadership of a congregation and the opportunities through RTF to see God transform lives, save marriages, and turn things around. All this could happen, simply by being a willing vessel, willing to do something crazy like uproot a family with small children and move across country based on the whisper of God.

As I reflect on the history of my ancestors, their stories of survival in the face of persecution and possible death, I do see parallels in my own life. In all the stories there is a sense of independence, and a willingness to uproot, and follow the voice of God to a new life. Only He, of course, knew the end from the beginning, and the story continues.

We all come from families and, in most cases, we carry the hurts and pain that came from growing up in those families. My father was definitely imperfect, as was my mother. But I've come to understand that I have a perfect Father that loves me totally and unconditionally. When I came to see just how good He is, and that He is the source of healing, forgiveness and true love, it changed me forever. Receiving the healing through Restoring the Foundations was life-changing. Nearly all the people that we have worked with as RTF ministers are believers in Jesus, many raised in the church. However, as we've said, "Hurt people, hurt people." So, whether it is parents that come from their own hurt and pain, or even religious leaders, we are all broken people in need of healing that only comes from Him. However, if He did it for me He can do it for you, as He has done for many that we have had the opportunity to help over these past ten years.

Maybe you believe in God, have accepted Jesus as your Savior, go to church and yet struggle with fear, rejection, shame and guilt. Or perhaps you are a Jewish person that has struggled just with the idea that there is a God at all. I get you; but more importantly, Jesus gets you. He is the source of life, love, peace and healing. We are here to help.

Because of Him, I have this incredible family, also made up of imperfect people, but joined together by the common experience of the Father's love through receiving and following the Messiah of Israel, Yeshua. You too can experience that love and be part of this family, with a perfect Abba Father. His arms are open wide, waiting for you and He will receive you just as you are.

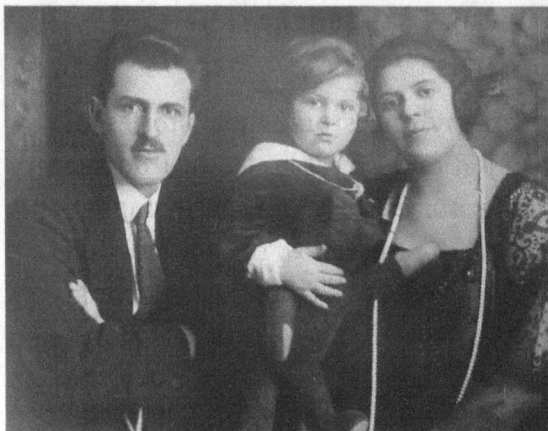

Grandma and Grandpa Brawer with Dad

Grandma and Grandpa
Scheidlinger with Mom

Steiger family reunion in Poland

My Dad, The Richie Boy

Mom and I, my chubby stage

Mom and Dad, Uncle Walter
and Aunt Hanna, war years

The Rabbi

The Athiest/Drug Dealer

Ira and Gloria Brawer

www.ingramcontent.com/pod-product-compliance
Lightning Source LLC
Chambersburg PA
CBHW010237100426
42813CB00012B/2639